PEPE ROMERO

La Guitarra

A COMPREHENSIVE STUDY OF
CLASSICAL GUITAR TECHNIQUE
AND GUIDE TO PERFORMING

TUSCANY PUBLICATIONS
TAMPA, FLORIDA

ISBN 978-0-9859451-0-7
(ISBN 10: 09859451-09)

TABLE OF CONTENTS

DEDICATIONS, INTRODUCTION, FOREWARD	6
THE RIGHT HAND	15
Awareness Exercises	15
The Nails	18
The Free Stroke	20
Chords and Arpeggios	24
The Plant	25
The Thumb	26
Giuliani: *Right-Hand Studies*	28
Rest Stroke	42
Exchange	43
Playing Without Nails	44
Diatonic Scales	44
Descending Scales	44
Pizzicato	45
THE LEFT HAND	46
Left-Hand Exchange	48
Left-Hand Pressure	49
Shifting Positions	50
Slurs (Hammers and Pull-Offs)	51
Vibrato	51
The *Barré*	52
Harmonics (Natural and Artificial)	53
Giuliani: *Left-Hand Studies*	55
GYMNASTIC EXERCISES	72
TREMOLO	84
Tárrega: *Improvisación: ¡A Granada! …*	
(Recuerdos de la Alhambra)	86
FLAMENCO	90
The *Rasgueado*	91
Pepe Romero: *Alegrías*	94
ESTUDIOS & COMPOSITIONS BY CELEDONIO ROMERO	99
Nana	101
Estudio No. 1: La Mariposa	102
Estudio No. 2	103
Estudio No. 3: La Abeja	104
Estudio No. 4	106
Preludio granadino (Variaciones)	107
Estudio No. 5: Preludio	110
Estudio No. 6: El Gaditano (Preludio)	112
Estudio No. 7: Estudio de concierto	114
Canción al alba No. 1	116
Canción al alba No. 2	118
Oración	120
THE CONCERT ARTIST	121
Automatismo	123
DEVELOPING VIBRATORY SENSE	126
THE METAPHYSICS OF MUSIC	127
A FINAL WORD	128
PHOTOS FROM THE ROMERO FAMILY ALBUM	129

*T*o my father, Celedonio Romero, the greatest guitarist in the world, who, with his magical playing and his profound sense of musicality, kindled the flame of love for music and the guitar that will burn eternally in my soul.　　　—Pepe Romero

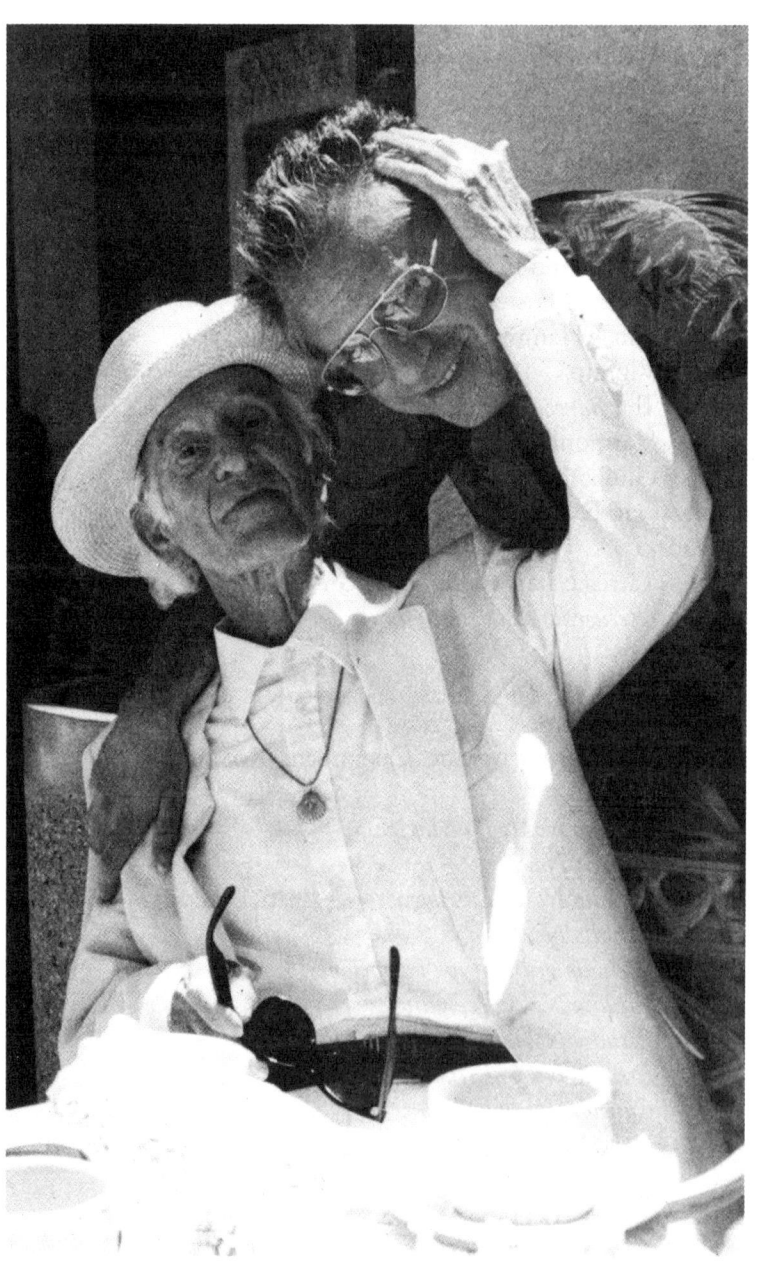

Dedications

To all my family—brothers, children, grandchildren—for enriching my life.

To Carissa, my wife, whose work and devotion provide me with the time, solace, and clarity to devote myself to my artistic endeavors.

To my daughter, Angelina Romero, for her precision in proofreading the original text and the music to prepare for this new edition.

To John King and Greg Shirer, for their assistance in proofreading.

To Susan Lamborghini, for the detailed notes she kept through many years of master classes which proved essential in preparing the first edition.

To Sandy Scheller, for her detailed and beautiful photographs for the new edition.

To my wonderful friend Lajos Markos, for the painting on the front cover and the wonderful artistic and musical evenings we spent together.

To Richard Long, for his assistance in making this new edition possible, but also for the opportunity it has given me to work with him and enrich our already profound friendship.

To Mary Long.

Introduction
to the First Edition

Dear Students, Brothers, and Sisters in the Divine Art of Music,

I speak to you from the depth of my heart so you may comprehend what motivates me to write this book on guitar technique. I will try to reveal my own experiences and interpret the teachings of the great masters of the past. My desire is that you find in yourselves the necessary spiritual strength to undertake, with joy and devotion, the technical discipline to which all serious students of music must submit in order to cross the invisible line that rigidly separates the dilettante from the artist.

It is not for the artist born complete and finished that I write, but for the one born with the love of music and troubled by the insufficiency of technical understanding that converts inspiration into frustration.

Through the considerable sacrifice required by intense technical study, and with a great love of music, the interpreter can attain that sweet ecstasy of transforming the notes that sleep in old manuscripts into sounds that live, and transport us along the path of fantasy to pure joy, taking us away from the problems and burdens of everyday life.

Flee from the illusion that one can achieve full participation in the art of music-making without engaging in the necessary technical study of the craft! It is my firm belief that he who walks onto a stage to perform a piece for which he is not prepared is equivalent to the executioner who kills an innocent victim. Study in great detail the teachings I give you, and abide by the following credo:

I will never perform a work for which I am not prepared, and every time I awaken a piece that is in repose, it will be to give it life, not death. Therefore, I will work with unceasing patience and devotion on my technical studies until I am worthy happily to awaken the sleeping melodies and unite my heart with that of the audience in the bond of the divine art of music.

—Pepe Romero (1981)

Foreword
to the New Edition

My earliest memories are of my father playing the guitar, and the many artists who frequented our home—painters, poets, writers, composers, the great Flamenco artists, and my father's colleagues—his contemporaries such as Narciso Yepes and Alirio Díaz, and the older generation of great guitarists who formed a bridge between him and the great Francisco Tárrega. They were the pupils of the great Maestro who, after the death of Tárrega in 1909, devoted themselves to passing on the teachings and memories they treasured, such as Daniel Fortea, Emilio Pujol, Josefina Robledo, and Rogelio Molina. They all took in the then young Celedonio Romero, and marvelled at his guitar playing and musicality.

In my memories, Rogelio Molina stands out, for he was the only living pupil of Tárrega whom I knew personally. He lived in Málaga and visited my father at least once a week. The visits would last all day and well into the night, and I remember tears running down the face of Don Rogelio as he listened to my father play. We all loved the stories he would tell about his beloved teacher and, many times, listening to Don Rogelio performing and demonstrating how Tárrega himself played. Don Rogelio was himself a wonderful guitarist. I am including the unedited letter from Rogelio Molina in which he described the profound effect the playing of my father (then twenty-four years old) had upon him.

As a teacher, my father was very patient and loving while, at the same time, very strict about us learning to play correctly. He taught us with incredible enthusiasm and infused in us his passion for the guitar. Our first contact with the guitar certainly began hearing him practice for hours when we were still in our mother's womb. He played the guitar for us when we were born and from early childhood, we grew up playing for his friends. My father was an extraordinary, magical being who lived and nourished himself from the poetry and mysticism of art. I treasure those memories, and the consequences they have had in making music an essential part of everything in my life.

My brothers, Celín and Angel, and I grew up feeling an enormous union that can never be broken. The guitar and music unified us with our father and mother in such a way that, wherever we are, we are together, branches of that same tree. My father used to tell us there was a single, great, immortal guitarist who played through the hands and hearts of all guitarists who, through the centuries, have devoted themselves, in body, mind, and soul, to music and the guitar. It warms my heart to see a third generation of Romeros, part of that genetic tree started by my father, continue to blossom in my nephews Celino and Lito, and through the magnificent guitars that my son Pepe has already given to the world. Now the Romero tree continues to flourish as a fourth generation—both boys and girls—as my grandchildren pledge their commitment to the guitar.

I hope this book will serve to help future generations of guitarists experience the great power and blessings of music. Let the guitar become the vessel that transports you to the depths of your inner being, connecting you with the cosmos and all of God's creation.   —*January 16, 2009*

Pepe Romero

Testimonial by Rogelio Molina,

Friend and Disciple of Francisco Tárrega
especially during the latter's stay in Malaga in 1899

Un alma de ángel, una sensibilidad engarzada de exquisiteces, una intuición extraordinaria y una técnica insuperable, se funden armoniosamente en Celedonio Romero, el eminente guitarrista, que, suave, plácido y místico cuando interpreta á Bach el coloso, enseñorea su inconfundible personalidad, mostrando las múltiples facetas de su arte en la ejecución depurada de las obras maestras del célebre Sors, de los clásicos inmortales y de los modernos compositores.

Yacía ya, dormido en el fondo de mi alma, el pasado recuerdo de las sabrosas enseñanzas del inmenso Tárrega y de mi entrañable amigo el insigne Miguel Llobet, en cuya intimidad cariñosa y juvenil tanto aprendí, identificándome con las dulzuras de ensueño y la transparencia inmaculada de su arte impecable .... Y, después de tantos años transcurridos, acallados los ecos evocadores de aquel ayer alegre y remoto, ha sido Celedonio Romero quien únicamente ha sabido despertar aquel recuerdo, haciéndome vibrar de entusiasmo, rememorando aquellos felices y lejanos tiempos y haciéndome sentir las mismas emociones de antaño.

Si mirarse en los ojos serenos é inocentes de un niño es buscar á Dios á través de su pureza, escuchar á Celedonio Romero en el recogimiento de sus recitales, es hallar en las regiones sublimes del Arte, sensaciones de espiritualidad selecta, deleite de sensibilidad que se adentra, como divino destello de ternura, en todos los corazones.

Admirable en su tecnicismo, fácil y seguro en la ejecución, sentimental hasta el romanticismo y fogoso hasta el ímpetu, domina con elegancia y delicadeza todos los secretos del instrumento, y es lógico que sepa esclavizar á su auditorio y adueñarse de todos los públicos. Pero posee también algo que no siempre acompaña á los virtuosos y que constituye el blasón del auténtico valer. Esta cualidad, es su modestia, innata en él, perdurable como una hostia sagrada, y tan sencilla y atrayente, que si le admiro como artista, igualmente le estimo por la honda bondad de su simpatía.

Auguro á Celedonio Romero, con la seguridad de percepción que me dan mis muchos años de estudio, un porvenir pletórico de éxitos resonantes, continuadores de los obtenidos en nuestra patria, llevando triunfalmente por toda Europa las sublimidades de su arte, encarnado en la dulce y poética, guitarra española.
Siempre invariable amigo y fervoroso admirador, con un efusivo y fraternal abrazo. Rogelio Molina 17-5-37

A soul of an angel, a sensibility adorned with exquisiteness, an extraordinary intuition, and an insuperable technique, all are harmoniously fused in the eminent guitarist Celedonio Romero. That gentle, placid mystic aristocratically displays his unmistakable personality when interpreting the colossal Bach, and demonstrates the multiple facets of his art in the purity of his execution of the masterpieces of the celebrated Sor and the immortal classical and modern composers.

Resting in the depths of my soul are my memories of the wonderful teachings of the eminent Tárrega and of my beloved friend, the distinguished Miguel Llobet, in whose youthful and loving company I learned so much, identifying myself with the sweetness of dreams and the immaculate transparency of his impeccable art .... And, after so many years passed, with the evocative echoes of that yesterday—happy, joyful and distant—having gone silent, it has been Celedonio Romero, the only one who has known how to awaken that memory, making me tremble with enthusiasm, recalling those happy and faraway times, and making me feel the same emotions of yesteryear.

If looking into the serene eyes of an innocent child is to see God through purity, to listen to Celedonio Romero in the intimacy of his recitals is to find in the sublime regions of the art sensations of spirituality, delight of the sensibility that penetrates—like a divine flash of tenderness—into all the hearts. Admirable in his technique, facile and sure in his execution, sentimental to the romanticism and fiery to the impetuosity, [he] dominates, with elegance and delicacy, all the secrets of the instrument, and it is logical that he knows how to enslave/capture his listeners and become the master of all audiences.

But he also possesses something that not always accompanies the virtuosos and that constitutes the blossoming of authentic worth. This quality is his modesty, innate in him, eternal as a Sacred Host, and so simple and attractive that, if I admire him as an artist, I equally esteem him for his deep goodness and charm.

I predict for Celedonio Romero, with the sureness of perception that my many years of study have given me, a future completely filled with the resounding success he has already attained in our country, and triumphantly continuing throughout all of Europe the sublimeness of his art incarnate in the sweet and poetic Spanish guitar.

His always unwavering friend and fervid admirer, with an effusive and fraternal embrace,

—Rogelio Molina, May 17, 1937

Celedonio Romero: Prelude No. 2, dedicated to Rogelio Molina
(Málaga, 1939)

Celedonio Romero, by Baldomero Romero Ressendi, 1941.

La Guitarra

A COMPREHENSIVE STUDY OF
CLASSICAL GUITAR TECHNIQUE AND
A GUIDE TO PERFORMING

Pepe Romero, age 12, in Sevilla.

*L*earn to study with the mental simplicity of a child, concentrating only on the problem that is to be overcome today and not bothering with that of tomorrow. In this way, you can find joy and self-assurance in conquering each problem, and every day you will be closer to the goal you are so earnestly seeking.

The Right Hand

One of the most difficult and important obstacles to overcome is the lack of knowledge concerning the internal feeling of the anatomy of both arms and, in particular, the forearms and hands. The lack of understanding of these feelings is the principal cause of tension, the villain whose treachery dominates so many unfortunate guitarists.

To overcome this tension, we will use a simple but very effective exercise which I call "Awareness." It consists of two parts:

1. Recognizing—while the hand is in a state of perfect relaxation—the key anatomical points at which the fingers will move, and the muscles that will affect these movements, and

2. Activating the movements while the other parts of the hands and forearms are left relaxed and undisturbed.

Gently put the *a* finger of the right hand on the first string, the *m* finger on the second string, the *i* finger on the third string, and the thumb on the fifth string. Close your eyes and visualize the right hand from the strings' point of view. Concentrate on how the different strings feel as they softly touch the tips of the fingers and the left corner of the nails. Memorize the respective thicknesses and tensions of each string. Also, develop an awareness of the fourth string between the index finger and the thumb, and of the sixth string over the thumb.

Without releasing the formation of the right-hand position, take the hand away from the strings by simply lifting the forearm (as if it were the tone arm of a record player) and recollect the experience of strings and fingers becoming one unit. When you have thought about this, put the hand back and check the accuracy of your memory. This should be repeated several times a day, until your recollection is always accurate.

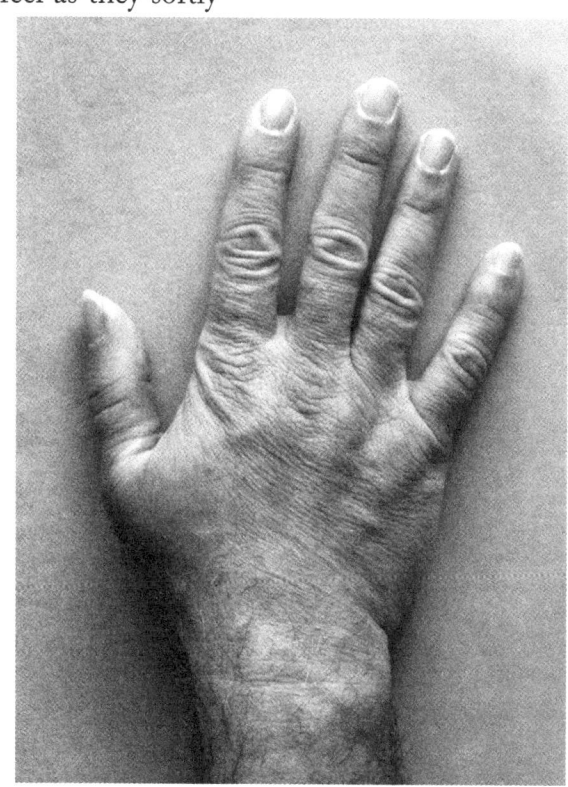

Figure No. 1

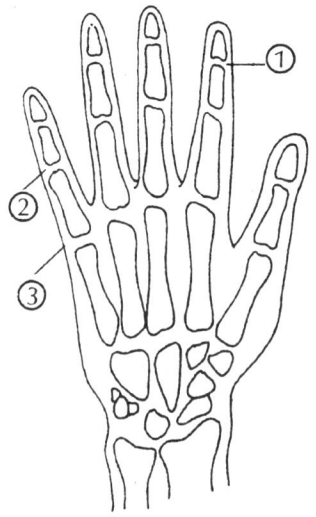

Figure No. 2 (above):
(1) Distal interphalangeal
(2) Proximal interphalangeal
(3) Metacarpo-phalangeal;

Figure No. 2a (below)

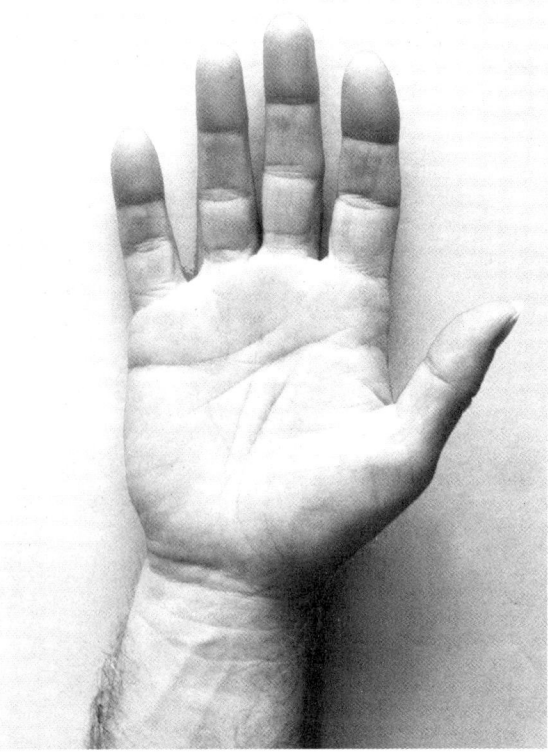

The point where the fingers and nails touch the strings must also always be consistent.

The second step of the awareness exercise uses the first finger of the left hand to touch softly the metacarpo-phalangeal joint of the index finger of the right hand. In order to describe most accurately and simply some of the movements made by the fingers, I will refer to the exact points of reference by their scientific names, as in *Figure No. 2.*

This will bring attention to the point from which the finger will be fired at the desired moment. You must then bring to mind the sound of the third string; the desire to hear that note must serve as the gunpowder to fire the index finger with velocity, weight, and relaxation in the direction marked in the picture. Once the finger has been fired and the sound made, the finger must be allowed to follow through as far as the initial shot will take it, without reaching the palm of the hand.

The same procedure must be followed with *m*, and *a* and thumb.

After this exercise has been practiced sufficiently, it will not be necessary to touch the metacarpo-phalangeal joint with the left hand; the final step is practicing the movement while placing the consciousness only at that point. Great care should be taken that the direction in which the fingers move is always constant and towards the point marked on *Figure No. 2a.*

This exercise is designed to help acquire independence between the fingers and eliminate tension, since tension is usually the result of being unable to feel and recognize the necessary muscles before they are flexed. Since tension can completely debilitate a player, a few more words should be added.

No muscle will tense by itself without having the necessary energy sent from the brain, whether sent consciously or subconsciously. Trying to stop tension at its muscular location is wrong and inefficient; you must stop it in the mind before it can become a thought.

The way to carry this out is through absolute and undisturbed concentration focused exclusively on the sound to be produced and on the feeling of the parts of the anatomy necessary to materialize that sound. If any thought is given to any other part of the body, it will result in tension at that point.

Trying to stop tension at the muscle involves another thought—another message from the mind to the muscle that can easily result in even more tension, ultimately distracting from the music itself. The correct procedure to eliminate tension is to stop, collect your mind, and try again, this time concentrating with all your power on only the parts of the body necessary to produce the sound, and becoming completely unaware that any other part of you exists.

Envision a triangle, with the upper point representing the thought of the desired sound, the lower left point the necessary feeling in the left arm and hand, and the lower right point the feeling in the right hand and fingers. Divide your energy equally among the three points exclusively, not allowing any other thought to enter your mind. Then the desire for the sound will serve as electricity to illuminate the center of the triangle, which will become a perfect circumference from which the materialized sound appears.

The
Nails

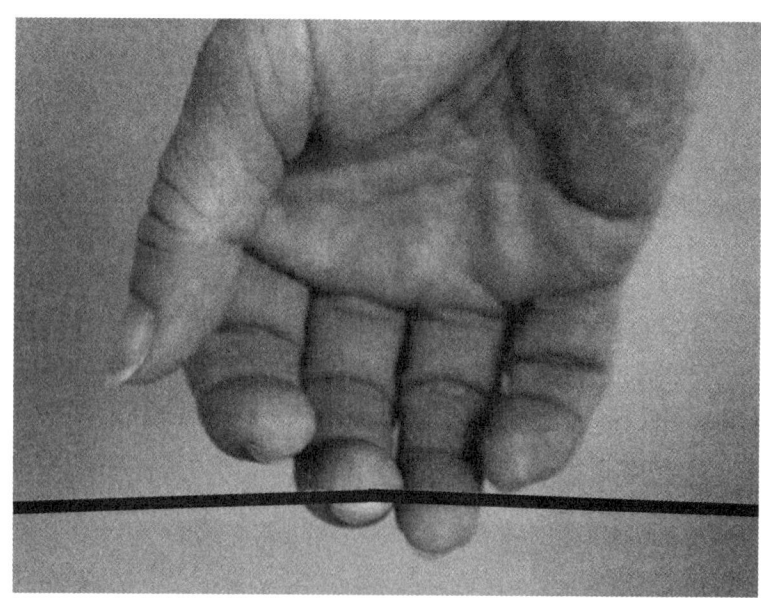

Figure No. 3:
Bright (above),
Darkest (below).

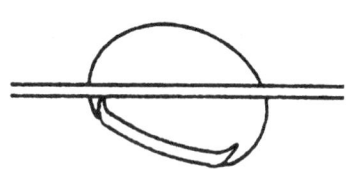

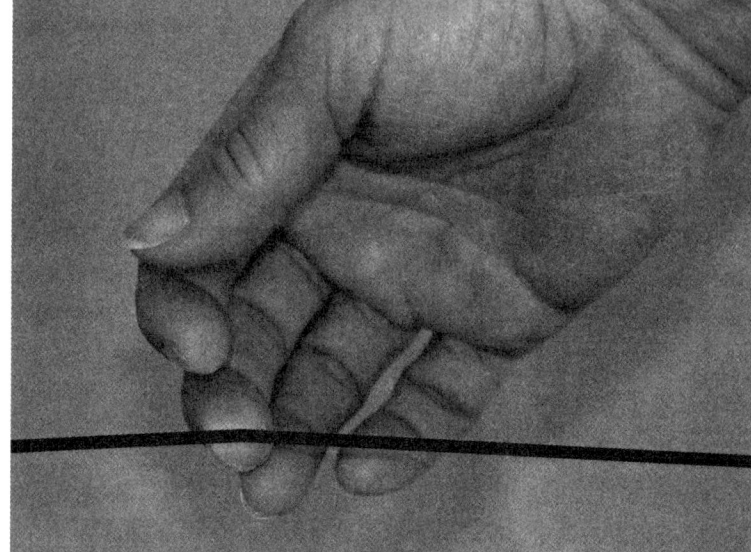

The various ways in which the fingertips and nails release the strings and the direction in which the strings are let free to vibrate should be the principal controlling factors for the color and quality of sound.

Much too often, guitarists depend upon plucking at different points along the string length to achieve tonal changes. That should be reserved for very definite color changes; it does not work in voicing. However, if the guitarist is skillful in achieving the subtle variations of plucking within one position, a tremendous variety of color can be achieved and separate notes can have different qualities simultaneously.

By varying the amount of flesh related to nail used when plucking the string, a great diversity of color can be produced from the same point on the string (see *Figure No. 3*).

Also, the more you move a string down toward the top of the guitar before setting it in vibration, the fatter and more velvety the sound will be. Conversely, the more parallel to the top of the guitar a string is pulled, the thinner the sound will be. These are the very basic differences; many more subtle changes in the strokes will result from lengthy experimentation by each and every player for himself.

The manner of shaping the fingernails is also very personal, for no two players have the same exact shape of nails, fingertips, fingers, hands and forearms. Any variation in any part of the playing mechanism results in compensation with the shape of the nail. However, there are some basic principles for shaping the nails. The nail is going to play on a string that is perfectly straight and it will touch the string at an angle. Therefore, when shaping the nail, we should duplicate that angle (between the nail and the string) in the angle between the nail and the flat surface of the shaper. In this way, the nail will be shaped to fit perfectly against the string.

At the point where the stroke begins, the edge of the nail should be sharp and at the point where it leaves the strings, the edge should be round. The first shaping is for grip and the second is for ease in sliding off (see *Figure No. 4*).

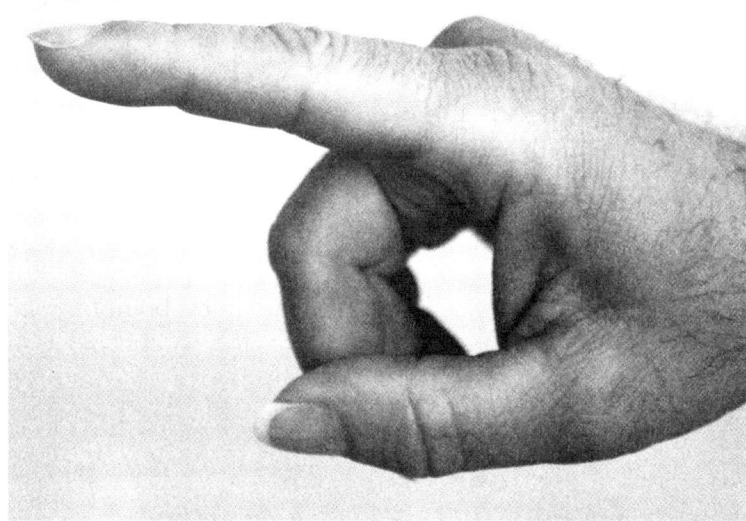

stroke begins

stroke ends

Figure No. 4

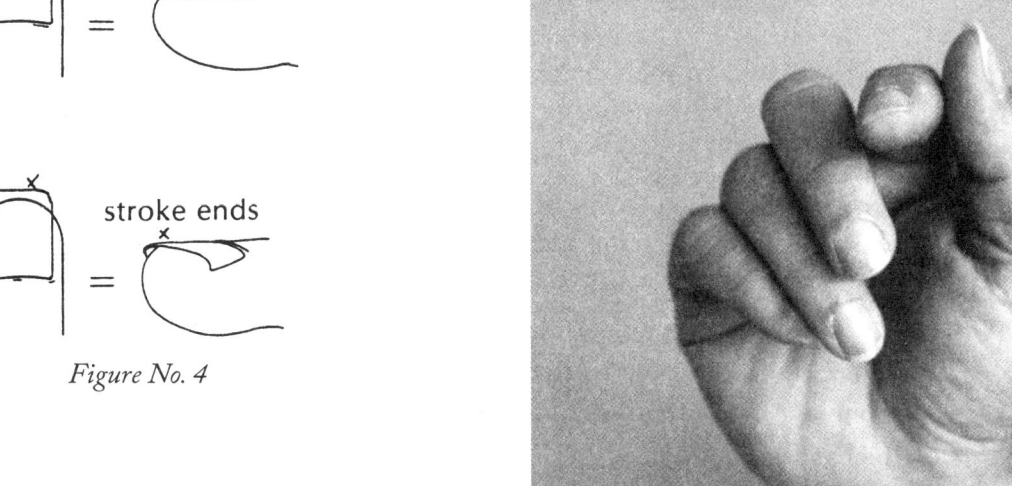

The more curved a nail is, the straighter it should be shaped. (see *Figure No. 5*).

The flatter the nail, the more pointed it needs to be (see *Figure No. 6*).

The more tapered the fingertips, the shorter the nail needs to be shaped (see *Figure No. 7*).

The fatter and more ball-like the fingertip, the longer the nail needs to be (see *Figure No. 8*).

The way in which nails are shaped also varies from finger to finger in the same hand.

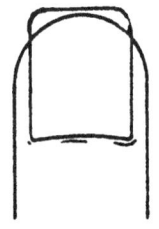

Figure No. 5

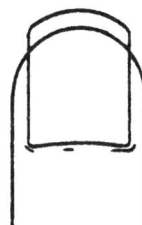

Figure No. 6

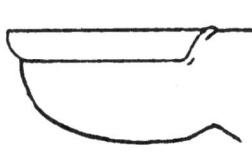

Figure No. 7

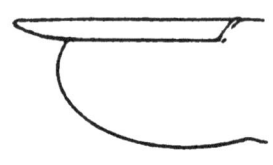

Figure No. 8

The Free Stroke

The master guitarist and composer, Gaspar Sanz, wrote concerning the right hand in his book *Instruccion de musica sobre la guitarra española y metodo de sus primeros rudimentos hasta tañerla con destrera:*

> *The fingers must not scratch the strings as many players do, but instead police your fingers well so that they do not exceed the necessary force for the desired sound.*

> *Take care that the fingers are well distributed among the strings.*

If we were to analyze these ideas and follow them consistently, most of the common problems would automatically disappear from the right hand.

By "not scratch[ing]" the strings, Sanz means that contact with the string must be established before setting it in vibration. By not exerting more force than necessary for the desired sound, you will develop an understanding of what, in my opinion, is one of the most important ideas in guitar technique—the association between the ear and the hands. In the end, it is the sound one desires that should trigger, motivate, and guide every movement the hands make.

To distribute the fingers well among the strings, it becomes necessary to plan and coordinate every move, maintaining complete independence of movements among the fingers and articulating them in the most efficient way from position to position.

Fernando Sor goes on to say, in his *Method for the Spanish Guitar:*

The lines on which the strings bear at the edge of the bridge is a straight line, as well as that of the nut. Consequently, all the strings are in the same plane. If these strings were to be touched by keys or moved by quills like the old harpsichords and spinets, all the hammers or jacks (when not in motion) would be seen to form a straight line parallel to the strings which they were to set in vibration and, when several were made to act at once, they would always preserve a straight line parallel to the plane of the strings. This would be one cause of uniformity in the quality and quantity of the sound. From this truth I deduce that it is necessary for the ends of the fingers of this hand to be placed in a straight line in front of the strings and parallel to the plane which they form.

The act of setting the string in vibration ought to be only the act of shutting the hand without shutting it entirely. The thumb should never be directed towards the hollow of the hand, but act with the next finger as if going to make a cross with it going itself above the finger.

The manner of setting the strings in vibration I began by establishing a principle which nobody can dispute, namely, that a stretched string as soon as any agent whatever causes it to quit the straight line towards which it is strongly impelled by its tension, if that agent ceases to prevent it, will fly towards it with an impetuosity which will carry it beyond the line on the opposite side. This deviation will, in its turn, produce a similar effect, this alternation continuing in proportion to the difference between the force of impulsion received and its tendency to repose. I should, therefore, consider my finger as an agent which moves it from its natural position and that the direction in which my finger moves it will determine that of its reaction.

Fernando Sor. (1778-1839) after Contemporary Portraits by Danny Shoemaker, 1994

From the writings of Sor we can clearly understand the importance of playing from the string in contrast to playing away from (or striking at) the string. If the string is touched immediately before making the sound, you kill the sound of the already vibrating string, thus hearing the beginning and the end of every note very clearly. Only then can one have control of how the string is to vibrate. Also, controlling how far the string is moved away from the line of repose determines the quantity of sound produced; the direction in which it is allowed to vibrate determines the color and quality of the tone. To produce a large sound, the fingers should release the strings with velocity and weight, not strength and force.

One of the most important things to understand before discussing the right- hand position and the free stroke is where the stroke actually originates. The finger should be made to move freely as a result of the impulse it is given by the forearm and the palm of the hand. The forearm is the place where the thought of the sound to be produced is transformed into energy. Then, the conciousness must be placed in the palm, and from there the signal is sent to the finger tip, which acts as a sensitive receiver. It is at the finger tip that the energy to set the string in vibration is given direction.

When you place your fingers on the strings, they must be loose and relaxed, since the very first contact with the strings generates the impulse in your finger. The finger must never be hard or stiff.

Finding the correct position for the right hand has everything to do with the anatomical makeup of every player and, therefore, the final position will be different with each player. The principles upon which to establish your own correct position, however, can and should be constant. For the free stroke, the *m* finger should act as the pivoting point upon which the palm of the hand should tilt to the left or the right. For players having a shorter *a* finger than *i*, the right side of the palm should be closer to the top of the guitar; if the *i* is shorter than the *a*, the left side of the palm should be closer to the top of the guitar; if they are the same length, the palm should be parallel to the top of the guitar. The height of the wrist is determined by the relative length of the thumb to the fingers.

The tilt of the hand should be achieved by rotating the forearm from the elbow, and not by forcing the wrist into an uncomfortable position that may impede the even flow of energy into the fingers.

The correct curvature of the fingers will also differ from player to player. To discover the proper curvature for yourself, place the tips of your fingers on a flat surface and then curl your fingers into your palm. The tips of your fingers should be even. Then turn your hand over and begin to uncurl them. As soon as the index finger becomes straighter than the middle finger, your hand is too open. *All fingers should have the same curvature and the fingertips should be even. (See Figure No. 9 on the following page).*

Another way to determine the proper curvature of the fingers for all free strokes is to make a fist, hold it tightly, then relax completely. When the hand is completely relaxed, the fingers will be in the correct position.

Each finger's curvature should be maintained throughout a stroke. (There is one small exception: each time a finger plays—touches the string, applies pressure and releases it—a small shock is produced. This shock must be absorbed by the flexibility of the distal interphalangeal joint, which gives at the moment the initial pressure is being applied. If this joint is instead held stiff and rigid, a harsh tone is produced.) If the hand is too far away from the strings, the fingers will have to straighten out to reach them, making the stroke awkward and resulting in a pinched sound. Having the hand too open impedes the flow of energy, and a great amount of strength is lost as a result.

In all playing, the motions of plucking the strings should be all in the fingers and not in the palm or arm. The right hand should not bounce with the movements of the fingers, nor should it be moved away from the strings during the fingers' strokes by lifting the forearm or bending the wrist.

When the correct curvature has been established, we still have to find how much of an angle the fingers must make in relation to the string. That is determined by the shape of the fingertip. The rule is this: Both nail and flesh must have contact with the string for the duration of the stroke. Once determined, the angle of the fingers relative to the strings should remain the same when playing treble or bass strings, with the forearm changing position to keep the hand placed correctly.

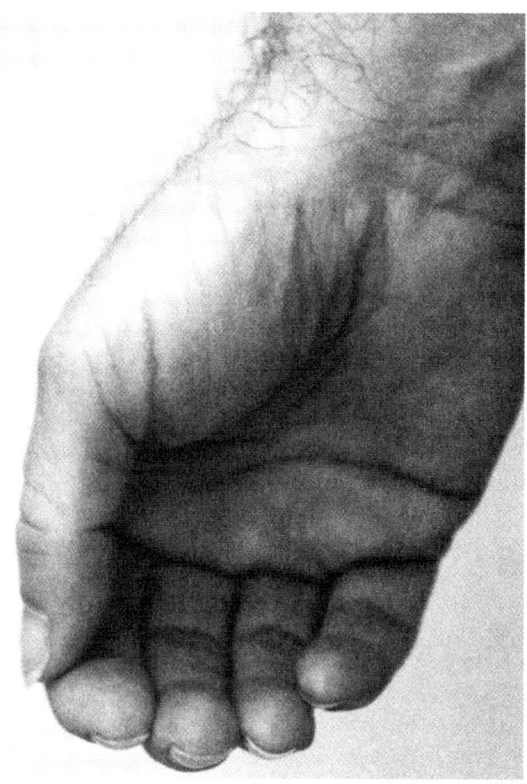

Figure No. 9

When the finger first makes contact with the string, it must be at the tip of the finger with the left corner of the nail touching the string. (Only in very rare cases have I found a hand anatomically suited to originate the stroke on the right side of the nail. In most cases, it causes too much bend in the wrist, forcing the index and anular (ring) fingers to play with different curvatures, and, as a result, with added tension and a considerable drop in speed. The nail should leave the string at the point where it curves back toward the finger (see *Figure No. 10*).

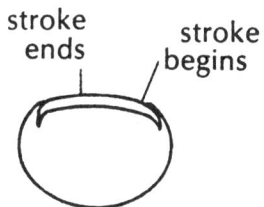

Figure No. 10

When playing chords or arpeggios, we must be very careful to maintain an orbit or trajectory that is always constant; the only variation should be in the size of the orbit, in order to achieve the desired dynamic quantity of sound. When I speak of the orbit or trajectory in which the fingers move, it is with the idea that the initial impulse that causes the finger to release the string and set it in vibration is the same impulse that brings the finger back again to playing position, without ever reversing the natural movement of the finger. If your hand is relaxed and you follow through on your free stroke, the finger will return in a circular path to its starting point completely on its own.

I cannot overemphasize the following word of caution: Do not exaggerate the follow-through. It is almost more dangerous to continue the movement of a finger toward the palm beyond the point where the original impulse carries it as it is to stop the finger from following through as soon as the string is played. The follow-through must be a natural and relaxed part of the total movement of the stroke. Always start the orbit not more than half a centimeter away from the string it is to play.

Chords and Arpeggios

When playing chords, move all the fingers as a unit, as though they were one finger. One impulse of energy should be distributed evenly among the fingers involved, leaving the fingers not in use at rest and undisturbed. After plucking a chord, all the fingers should end in the same position relative to each other as when planted on the strings before plucking; no one finger should overtake the others. Also, the fingers should be kept close to the strings they are to pluck and never should be thrown out too far before plucking; the palm should not move, as this will further throw the fingers out of position.

The desired goal and inevitable result of all this planning, if it is carried out exactly and properly, is for all the fingers to be completely independent of one another. In both the inner part of the orbit (the plucking and follow-through) and in the outer part of the orbit (the return of the finger to its resting position, again half a centimeter in front of the string it will play next), the movement of each finger should be carried out entirely without influencing or being influenced by the movement of any other.

If you break down an arpeggio, finger by finger, and look at the period of time taken by each finger to repeat its cycle, it is evident that there is a lot of time to play the stroke, relax the finger, return to the string and play again. If the fingers are completely independent of one another, they will use as much time as possible (*i.e.*, the time between two notes played by the same finger) to return to the string. In this way, maximum speed is achieved through minimum effort.

When playing arpeggios or tremolos, the single most important principle is to have each finger at a different point in its orbit—in other words, to have one finger in flight during the follow-through, another returning to find the string it must play next, and another touching the string that is to sound next. If you were to take a movie of a perfect arpeggio and stop the action, the above description would apply.

A very easy and practical way to achieve this independence is to practice a circular motion away from the guitar (like pedaling a bicycle between *i* and *m*, *m* and *a*, and *i* and *a*).

When playing groups of notes such as arpeggios, all notes in the group are released from your mind into your body as a single thought, letting your body distribute the notes in the proper rhythm. As you "watch" each group play, your mind is putting together the next thought.

"Full plant" is the name of the technique in which two or more fingers rest on the strings they are to play (as if to play a chord) but instead play them one at a time. For example, in the Giuliani Right-Hand Studies (below), see Mauro Giuliani's Arpeggio No. 2 (*p, i, m, p, i, m, etc.*): *p* will play; at that moment *i* and *m* position themselves on the respective strings they are to play; *i* will play, *m* will play. During the *i* and *m* strokes, *p* has made its way back, via a small circular motion to the string it is to play, and the complete process is repeated.

The full plant is not only usable but highly recommended in most ascending arpeggios that start with *p*, such as Nos. 2, 4, 7, *etc.* When the thumb and a finger start off the arpeggio playing together, the full plant does not work, even though the arpeggio may be an ascending one, for the fingers need the period of time during which the thumb plays to return to playing position before they can plant. (for example: arpeggio No. 11)

In an arpeggio starting with the thumb, in which the first few notes are ascending and the end of the group is descending, we can use the full plant only for the ascending part. For example: No. 31 (*p, i, m, a, m, i*) *p* plays as *i, m* and *a* plant; *i* plays; *m* plays; *a* plays; *m* plays; *i* plays and the complete process is repeated.

"Sequential plant" is the name of the technique in which a finger touches the string it is going to play and rests there for an instant before playing it. This technique is wonderful training to make the fingers play from the strings. It is highly recommended when practicing all arpeggios, both ascending and descending. During actual performance, however, the sequential plant will be subconscious.

Example: The arpeggio in Giuliani's *Right-Hand Study No. 3* (*p, m, i*): as *p* plays, *m* reposes on the string; as *m* plays, *i* reposes on the string; as *i* plays, *p* reposes on the string; then the circle is repeated.

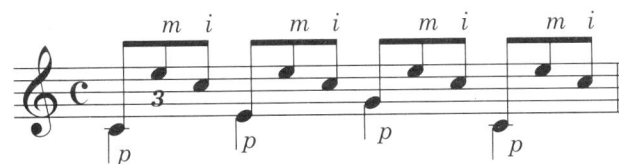

The Thumb

The right-hand thumb plays very much as the fingers do, completely independent of the rest of the hand. The thumb, like the fingers, plays with nail and flesh touching the string simultaneously. But because it plays at about a forty-five degree angle to the string, it can also play with the flesh only or with the nail only (provided the nail is shaped correctly) to achieve different tonal qualities. At its contact with the string, and throughout its stroke, the thumb should be extended and not held in close to the hand (this also applies to the thumb's free stroke).

Unlike the fingers (which should be thoroughly trained in the free stroke before attempting the rest stroke), I believe in training the thumb in the rest stroke from the beginning. The use of the rest stroke allows the thumb to maintain its support on the bass strings, serving as an anchor for the three fingers and giving stability to the entire hand. You should always feel the counterbalance of the fingers in relation to the thumb; this will further stabilize the complete hand and will insure that you play by moving the fingers and not the hand. This counterbalancing and stabilizing feeling is most apparent when using a full plant with the fingers.

In the rest stroke, the entire thumb moves, not just the first joint. Although it is stopped by the next string, the stroke should be envisioned as a long one. Do not think of the motion as being just from one string to the next, but carry the motion through in your mind.

Now let's examine the most common problems that occur in the thumb rest stroke and discuss the solutions:

DROPPING TO THE NEXT STRING:
When the thumb drops to the next string (for example, landing on the fifth string after plucking the sixth with a rest stroke), too much of its flesh will be touching the string to be able to play immediately from that position and produce a good tone.

To correct this, you must relax the thumb and allow the pressure of the string to propel it (like a trampoline) to the correct position from which it can then play.

SKIPPING STRINGS:
For an example of this problem, suppose the thumb plays the sixth string and must go directly to the fourth. In this case, we again use the trampoline effect but in a larger form. When the thumb plays, it meets with the fifth string; the resistance of that string changes the direction of the thumb's force and momentum, causing it to lift off the fifth string in the opposite direction from which it came. When the player feels this, he should guide the thumb into a small circular path that carries the thumb on to the fourth string (see *Figure No. 11*).

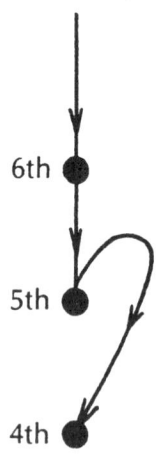

Figure No. 11

6th
5th
4th

RETURNING TO A LOWER STRING:

Suppose you have just played the fifth string and the thumb has to go back to the sixth string. Once again we have the trampoline effect of bouncing off the fourth string, up over the sixth string in a circle and coming down on the sixth string (see *Figure No. 12*).

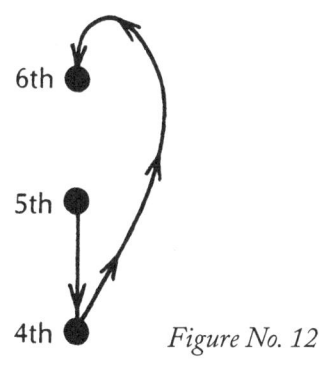

6th
5th
4th   *Figure No. 12*

The free stroke of the thumb is very much like that of the fingers. The follow-through and the circular motion of the stroke are just as important in changing the direction of the stroke from the downward motion of just having played to the upward motion of returning the thumb to play again.

Let's examine the various possible sequences of strings the thumb is most likely to encounter:

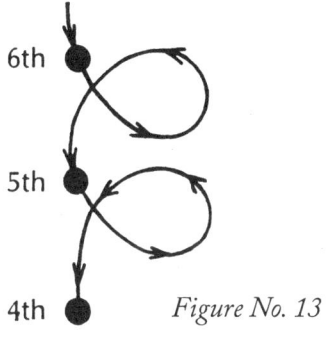

6th
5th
4th   *Figure No. 13*

1. Playing the sixth, fifth, and fourth strings consecutively (see *Figure No. 13*).

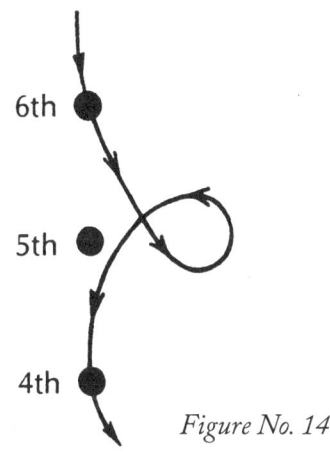

6th
5th
4th
          Figure No. 14

2. Skipping strings, ascending; the motion is the same as in No. 1, but the circle is slightly larger (see *Figure No. 14*).

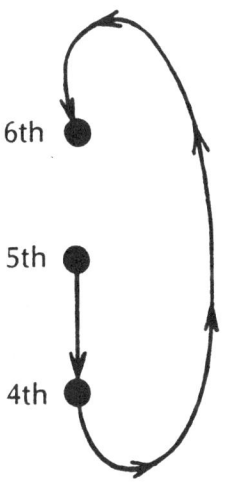

6th
5th
4th

          Figure No. 15

3. Returning to a lower string (see *Figure No. 15*).

Giuliani Right-Hand Studies

It is with the deepest respect and admiration for one of the greatest masters the guitar has ever had, Mauro Giuliani (1781-1829), that I present his *120 Right-Hand Studies* (from his guitar method, Op. 1, of 1812). Not only has this great genius left us an incredible wealth of music, but he has also left us the "formulas" by which to play them. To this day I hold them as an indispensable part of my training.

To prevent discomfort in the left-hand index finger, I have arranged the studies so that they alternate between the keys of C and A major.

The feeling of unity should never be lost through a tendency to concentrate on the composite groups of notes. When playing groups, all the notes in the group are released from your mind into your body as a single thought, letting your body distribute them in proper rhythms. As your body experiences each group, your mind prepares the next.

STUDIO
per la
Chitarra
— DI —
Mauro Giuliani

Opera Prima

a Vienna presso Artaria e Comp.

N.º 2246

Giuliani Right-Hand Studies

Edited and Revised by Pepe Romero

Mauro Giuliani

29

30

31

33

34

36

39

40

41

The Rest Stroke

The rest stroke with *i, m,* or *a* has only very subtle differences in hand position from that of the free stroke. The player should be able to change from one to the other with a very small variation in position; otherwise, it becomes difficult and awkward to use a rest stroke to accent a note within a free stroke passage.

The rest stroke should not differ in tonal quality from the free stroke; a player should be able to interchange free and rest strokes without an audible difference.

Figure No. 16a (top): the index finger begins the rest stroke; Figure No. 16b (below): the index finger completes the rest stroke.

In a single-note passage using rest strokes only, a slightly higher wrist position (compared to that used with free strokes) is allowable.

The major difference between the rest stroke and free stroke is in the amount of flexing in the distal interphalangeal joint. Be careful of when and how much you flex. The flexing should serve as a shock absorber. If it happens the moment the sound is produced, the string will be plucked slower and the tone will be mushy and out of focus.

The correct way to flex is this: As you begin to apply pressure to the string, the interphalangeal joint gives a little. Then, when you release the string, the joint regains some of its strength.

When alternating *i* and *m,* the *m* flexes more than *i* to compensate for the difference in their lengths, and is slightly more curved when it plays. The *m* finger also flexes more when executing the rest stroke than it does in the free stroke.

When the fingers are resting and facing the strings they are to play, they should be about three millimeters (3 mm.) away from the strings, not on them. When they do touch the strings, they should feel stretched ever so slightly.

When alternating *m* and *a,* the *a* plays in the same manner as *i;* when *i* and *a* play in alternation, their movements are very much alike.

What you do with the fingers not in use during these maneuvers is of great importance. I have found when using *i* and *m* (the most popular alternating combination), *a* should be tucked into the palm about one centimeter (1 cm) more than *m*. When alternating *i* and *a*, the *m* finger should be carried about one and a half centimeters (1.5 cm) out from the other fingers; when alternating *m* and *a*, the *i* should be about even with *m*.

By keeping the unoccupied finger in these respective positions, the center of balance of the palm remains more even and, therefore, frees the working fingers to play with greater ease and facility.

It is also important to try and rest the thumb on a bass string whenever possible, to feel the same counterbalance of which I spoke earlier (see The Thumb, above). This time, however, we feel it primarily in the fingers.

When playing rest strokes on the bass strings, the thumb may slide against the top of the guitar very gently. It should be in such a position that, when *i* and *m* are alternating on the sixth string, they may come to rest against the thumb as if it were a seventh string.

As I said earlier when discussing the free stroke, the fingers should play from the string, not with a slapping motion of the fingers but in a "touch–pressure–release" sequence. This practice affects a perfect coordination between both hands, a point I will elaborate upon when discussing the left hand.

Exchange

There should be an exchange of motion between alternating fingers. When a finger plays with a rest stroke, it must have a perfect follow-through, letting the resting string stop it. Against this resting string, the finger maintains the weight with which it landed until, at the exact moment the next finger plays, it relaxes and lets the string propel it to its next playing position. I call this maneuver "exchange." It should be perfectly synchronized—the fingers pass each other over the string on which they are alternating, both being activated by the same thought.

Be careful that the motion of the fingers is constant in their return to playing position, not more than five millimeters (5 mm.) away from the string each will play next.

Always travelling the same distance before encountering the string immensely improves the relationship and friendship between fingertip and string.

Playing Without Nails

To develop this sensitivity, I recommend that all guitarists play without nails for a period of one year. My father, brothers and I all did this at an early age. I still remember asking my father, "When can I grow my nails?" after I was playing on my fingertips for a few months. He answered, "When your fingertips and the strings become one." At the time I did not enjoy hearing that, but now I thank him for it.

Diatonic Scales

Practicing diatonic scales is essential for the development and maintenance of technique. Practice scales daily. In addition to even rhythms, practice them with the following rhythms:

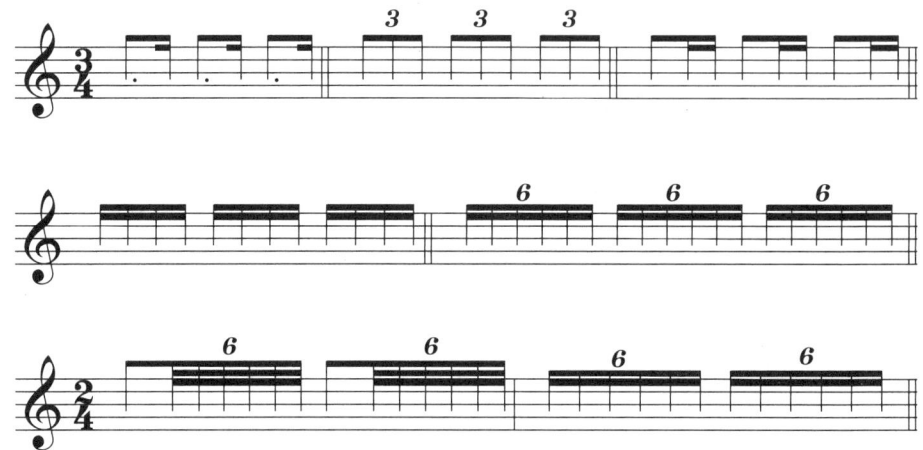

Scales should be practiced staccato, legato, and with dynamic variations—*crescendi, diminuendi, subito f, subito pp,* and any other dynamic changes your fantasy dictates, spontaneously, and without premeditation. When playing staccato, each note has its own energy, with a beginning and an end. In legato playing, all of the notes have a single, unbroken energy that unites each to the one that follows, as if each note gives birth to the next. This is accomplished by passing the energy from one finger to the other, as a ball is passed from one player to another in a soccer match.

Descending Scales

This technique in rest stroke playing is optional, although it is one that I use with great pleasure and success. It involves sliding the index finger on to the lower string as shown:

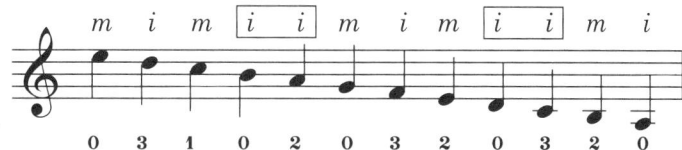

After playing the "b" on the second string, the index finger is not in perfect position to play the "a" on the third string. It will land with too much flesh. While keeping pressure on the string, roll the index finger until you feel the corner of the nail touch the string and it is in the correct position to release the string to vibrate. This maneuver must be done in one continuous, fast motion. When done well, it is very effective and easy.

Figure No. 17

Pizzicato

There are two major ways to play *pizzicato*, also known as *étouffée*. The most common is with the right side of the right-hand palm touching and muting the string by the bridge. The edge of the palm should be placed behind the saddle so that the player can vary the amount of flesh that goes over the saddle, thus controlling the quality of the *pizzicato* (see *Figures Nos. 17* and *18*).

The other method is to position the left hand fingers directly over the fret. This style of *pizzicato* is very effective when playing in high positions on the treble strings.

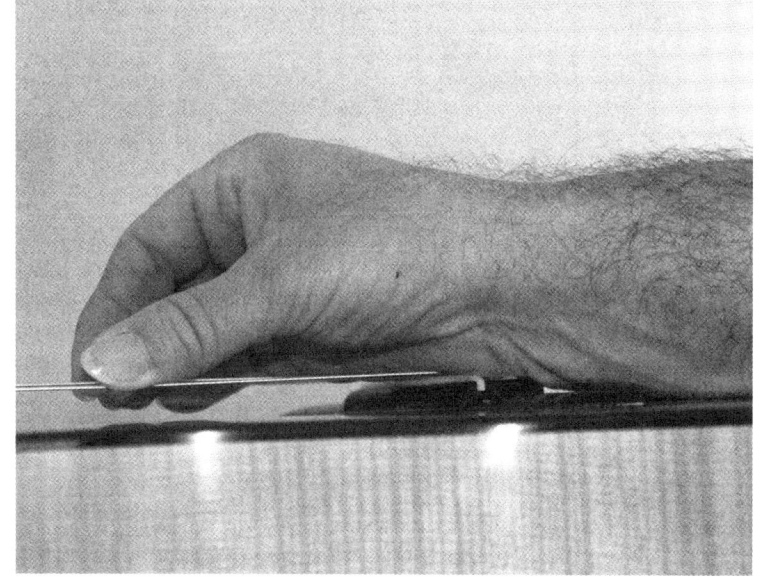

Figure No. 18

The Left Hand

Gaspar Sanz left us this instruction for the left hand: "The left hand must be applied with *garbo* (gracefulness, gentility and elegance of manner) and *vizarria* (confidence of movement) to the fingerboard, keeping the thumb as the tiller of this sonorous vessel."

I have always thought of the fingers of the left hand as five ballet dancers dancing beautifully on a stage (the fingerboard), and I cannot help feeling that Gaspar Sanz had a very similar image of the left hand when he referred to it with the terms "gracefulness, gentility, elegance" and "confidence". There is no better manner to describe the guitar than to call it a sonorous vessel, for the purpose of the guitar is none other than to transport those who play it, and those who listen, closer and closer toward finding happiness.

If we continue with the idea of the fingers being ballet dancers, we should train them as such. They must each know their parts independently of one another. The choreographer (the guitarist who decides on the fingering) must choreograph a piece to avoid clutter; one finger should not get in the way of another but should keep a smooth and beautiful flow of movement complimentary to the musical flow of a piece.

Fernando Sor tells us: "I saw no reason why the thumb, which plays such an important part in the right hand, should do nothing in the left hand ... I therefore began by supposing, as an established principle, that being shorter than the fingers, and having the power of acting easily in the opposite direction, it might be brought to meet them and offer a point of support for the neck."

This statement by Sor coincides perfectly with Gaspar Sanz's description of the thumb as the tiller. It indeed must be ready to accent and counterbalance the energy put out by the fingers at all times, and the fingers in turn must direct all their energy to the thumb. This balance is very much like a male dancer lifting up and supporting the female dancer.

The left hand should always approach the fretboard in a position that allows each finger equal access to every string; this usually means that the knuckles will be parallel to the strings. In this position, each finger will be able to move, for example, from the first string to the sixth without moving the hand or arm (see *Figure No. 19*).

The fingers should play close to the frets without covering them, for that would cause a *pizzicato* sound. When you play a note that does not sound good, freeze the movement and look at your left hand; see if the sound was caused by a bad finger position and, if so, try to correct it. Make sure you always press the string down with the same part of your fingertip; get the feeling of where the string should be under your finger. The complete weight of your fingers should go into the fingerboard. If the forces between your fingers and thumb are not balanced, the focus of the weight will not be correct and your fingers will not play with their full potential.

Another very important principle to remember is not to make sudden movements with your left hand, but to take all the time you have available between notes; all your movements must be graceful. We should think only of the fingers being used, removing all awareness and energy from the fingers that are resting. At the same time, any and all fingers should be able to position themselves over any given string with the same ease and comfort.

The fingers work in much the same way as do the legs when we walk—only one leg at a time supports your weight and the other leg, although moving to take the next step, is completely relaxed. Imagine how terribly difficult walking would be if both legs were equally tense at all times. The fingers have to work in exactly the same way; this relaxation of the fingers that are not holding down a string has a rejuvenating effect, adding greatly to the acquisition of endurance.

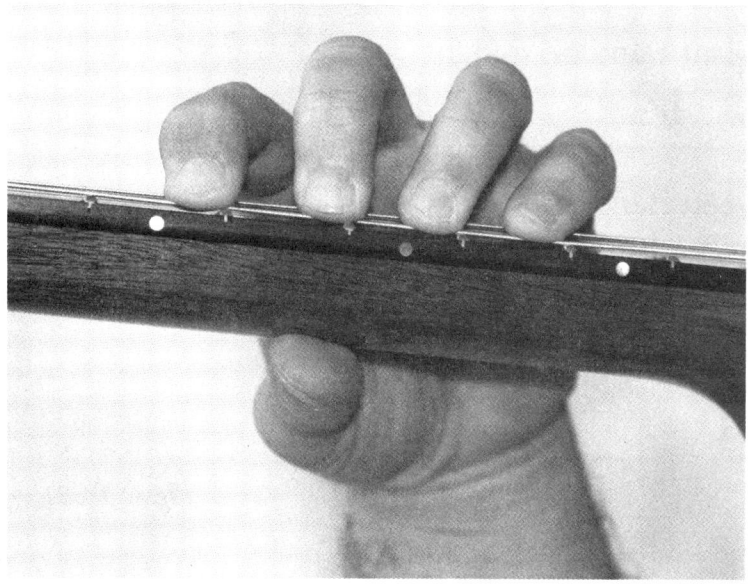

Figure No. 19

Left-Hand Exchange

The principle of exchange is as important to the left hand as it is to the right. At the moment a finger is released from holding down a string, energy is removed and given to the finger that has to play next. For example, when playing a chromatic scale, as the first finger plays, the second should be directly over the next fret, prepared to play. The next thought or impulse should simultaneously release the first finger, play the second, and prepare the third over the fret it is to play next. The next thought releases the second, plays the third, and prepares the fourth, and so on.

This exchange has to be coordinated and timed exactly with the right hand in the following order:

1. The string is touched exactly at the same time by the left and right hand fingers (see *Figure No. 20*).

2. Pressure is applied by both fingers, also at the same time (see *Figure No. 21*).

3. The left hand holds on while the right hand and finger let go of the string, setting it into vibration (see *Figure No. 22*).

These three steps are, of course, generated by one thought and are affected in one continuous motion. The movements of lifting the left-hand fingers off the strings and of placing the next fingers down have to be coordinated both in their velocity and timing.

To practice this you should play slowly but with velocity in your movements (*i.e.*, the time between notes can be great, but each note should be produced quickly with definite, not jerky, movements). When practicing slowly, you have plenty of time to direct your fingers in the right motions and to check them after each move to make sure they are playing properly.

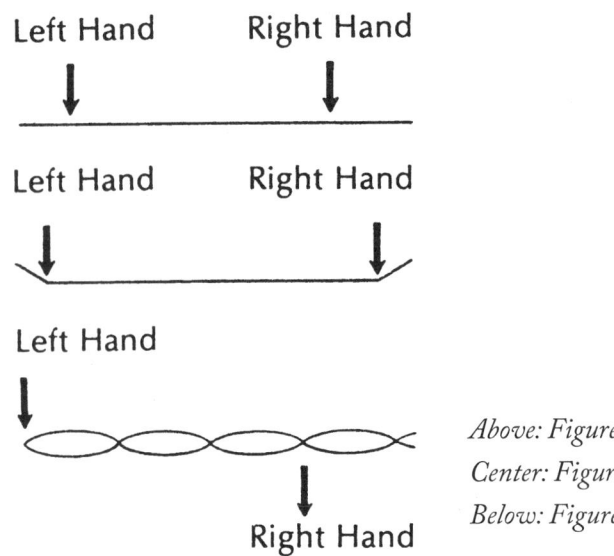

Above: Figure No. 20
Center: Figure No. 21
Below: Figure No. 22

The way in which the pressure is applied is most important. To add solidity to the left-hand fingers as they hold a chord, let the weight of the relaxed arm to be added to the pressure of the fingers. The arm should be held up by the pressure of the fingers and thumb so that if someone were suddenly to remove the guitar from your fingers, your left hand and forearm would drop. When the fingers shift position or release pressure on the neck, the arm is held up by its own power. This interchange offers both arm and hand a chance to rest intermittently.

Adding the weight of your arm also causes the fingers automatically to play perpendicular to the strings.

When shifting fingers, the thumb does not drastically change position; the only change is the direction in which the thumb's pressure is applied, and this depends on the change in finger configuration.

Releasing a left-hand finger from duty is done in the same manner as in the right hand, with the movement originating in the metacarpo-phalangeal joint, never allowing the proximal interphalangeal joint to open up completely. Then you will always be ready to play, consistently keeping the necessary curvature to your fingers.

Movement at the proximal interphalangeal joint leads the finger to find the proper string, and movement at the metacarpophalangeal joint brings the finger to touch the string. This second movement must be executed with velocity, letting the string stop the motion of the finger. The contact should be as between two trapeze acrobats—secure, with confidence and perfect timing.

The left-hand fingers should always play as if they are hammering, such that if you stop plucking with the right hand you should be able to hear the notes being hammered by the left hand. The same principle of the follow-through in the rest stroke of the right hand applies to the left: let the fretboard stop the motion of the finger in the same manner that the string stops a rest stroke. Make sure that the string is pressed straight into the fingerboard, not up or down, so that the strings are always the same distance apart on the fingerboard.

Left-Hand Pressure

Shifting Positions

When shifting from the fourth finger to the first in an ascending chromatic scale, the palm of the hand should contract, bringing the first finger close to the fourth as it plays. At the moment of the shift, the first finger takes its place at the next note as the hand relaxes and resumes its proper shape and placement. When playing a descending chromatic scale, the process of contraction and relaxation of the hand is the same; the only difference is that the fourth finger comes close to the first and then leads in the jump.

In order to avoid the string noise caused by sliding a finger along the string when shifting positions, the finger should move like a paint brush, finding the soft part of the finger to slide on, not the callous (see *Figure No. 23*). When changing chords, it is a good practice to try to find a finger common to the two chords, one that can be kept on the string and used as a guide. Precede the positioning of the new chord with your eyes and your mind, letting the hand realize the chord as it already exists in your imagination. When it is impossible to prepare your left-hand fingers to play the next note (*i.e.*, when a finger plays two notes in a row), your mind does the preparation. Your eyes and mind should focus only on the beginning and end of a shift, effecting it instantly. They should not be conciously aware of the move, only of the result. With the subconcious mind guiding the shift, every finger will automatically move in the shortest possible route.

Figure No. 23

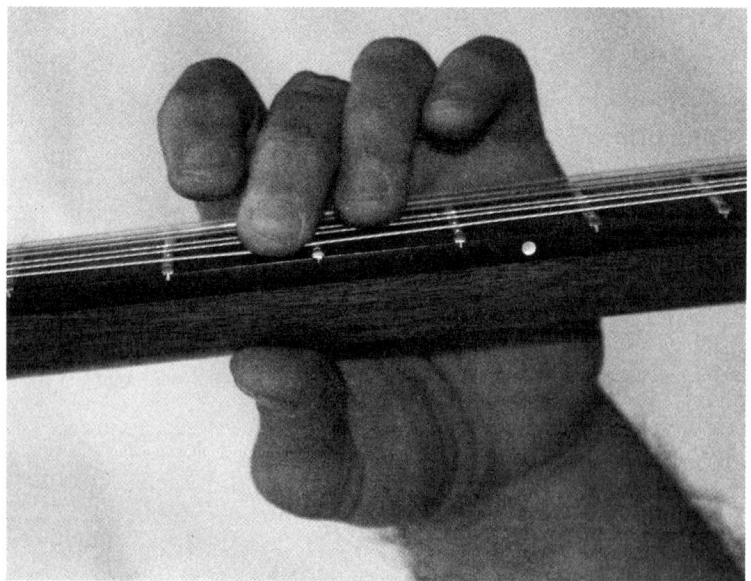

The hammer, or slurring of an ascending note, is played by the left-hand finger(s) in very much the same way they always play, except perhaps with slightly more force. The only difference is that the right hand does not pluck the string to set it in vibration; the string is set in motion by the force of the left hand hitting it as it frets the note. A strong, loud sound in an ascending slur comes from the velocity and definition of the stroke, not from strength or pressure.

The pull-off, or slurring of a descending note, is a little more complicated, since the left-hand fingers must set the string in motion much as the right-hand fingers do. After a note is played, the left-hand finger fretting that note plucks the string (moving parallel to the fretboard) to sound the slurred note.

In pull-offs, we also use free and rest strokes, with the free stroke being faster and the rest stroke sounding bigger, with a more definitive attack; everything I have said about the right-hand free stroke and rest stroke applies exactly to left-hand pull-offs.

There are two basic ways to play a *vibrato*. One is to move or vibrate the string up and down (vertically, perpendicular to the strings). The other is to move or vibrate it from side to side (horizontally; parallel to the strings).

The horizontal *vibrato* is the most common form and is definitely the preferred one for single notes from the fourth fret and up. This *vibrato* should be played by placing all the weight on the finger effecting the *vibrato*, removing all pressure, weight, and support of the thumb. As a matter of fact, in most cases when I use this type of *vibrato*, my thumb ceases to touch the neck of my guitar. The vibrating energy comes from the finger, hand and forearm.

The vertical *vibrato* is highly recommended in positions lower than the fourth fret, and in chords where the guitarist may wish to give *vibrato* to a single note without giving it to others. This movement originates at the proximal interphalangeal joint. The thumb, in this case, continues to play the same major role as in all other playing, offering its support, guidance and strength, especially to the finger effecting the *vibrato*.

The Barré

The thumb is perhaps the most important supporting point in the *barré*. The pressure on the fingerboard and neck should be equally divided between fingers and thumb with the barring first finger pressing most firmly between the proximal interphalangeal joint and the distal interphalangeal joint.

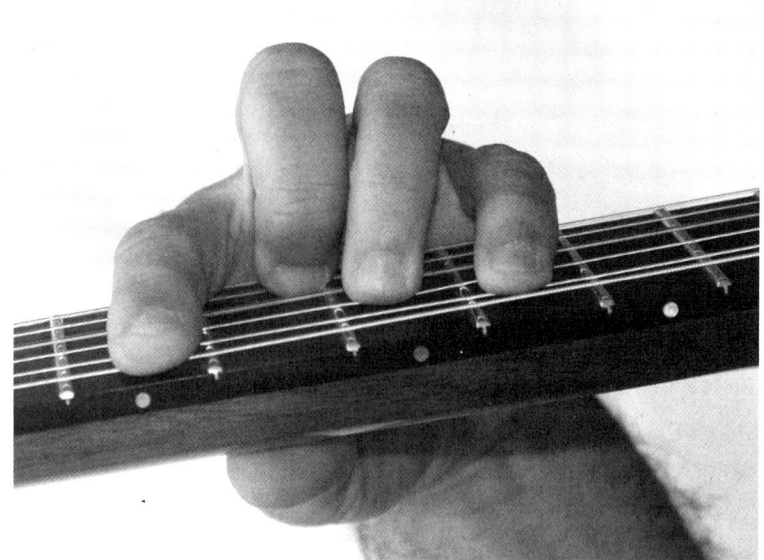

Figure No. 24

To add pressure to the *barré* without creating tension, roll the index finger toward the sound hole. Do not slide over the fret; keep the skin in the same place and simply roll the finger over. This also relaxes the other left-hand fingers.

Figure No. 25

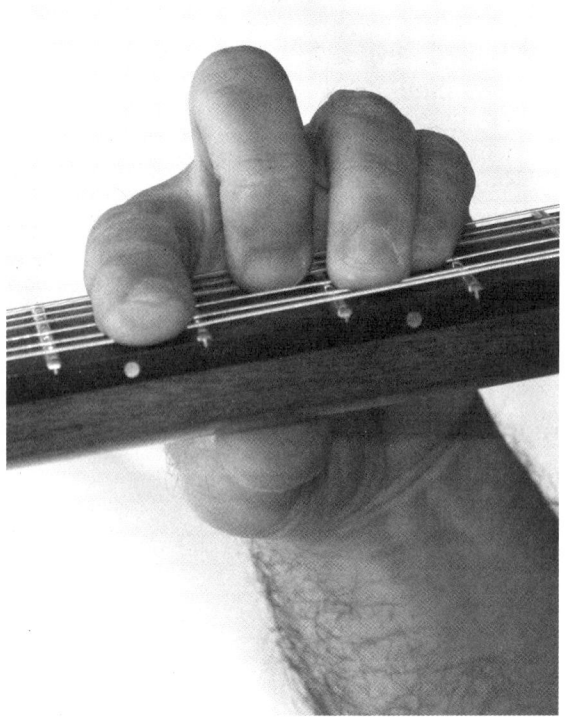

When barring without any other fingers down, the pressure of the thumb should be right behind the index finger. When other fingers are also holding notes, you must find the center of balance of all the fingers involved and direct the energy of the thumb to that point.

It is very important to strengthen the *barré* so that the other fingers are perfectly relaxed and able to move in any direction while the *barré* is being held (see *Figures Nos. 24–25*).

NATURAL HARMONICS

Natural harmonics are produced by touching the string directly over the fret very lightly with the left hand while plucking it with the right. Their production involves four major points:

1.) The pad of every finger has a point where the finger tapers to a more slender contour; this point is usually at the center of the whorl of the finger print. It is this part of the finger that should touch the string lightly. The purpose in using this point is to have as small a surface of the finger as possible in contact with the string (see *Figure No. 26*).

2.) As soon as the sound is made, the left hand finger should be gently removed from the string (see *Figure No. 27*).

3.) The right hand should pluck softly using a free stroke with much nail and little flesh.

4.) The proper place to pluck the string is at a point about two thirds of the string length from the left hand to the bridge of the guitar (see *Figure No. 28*).

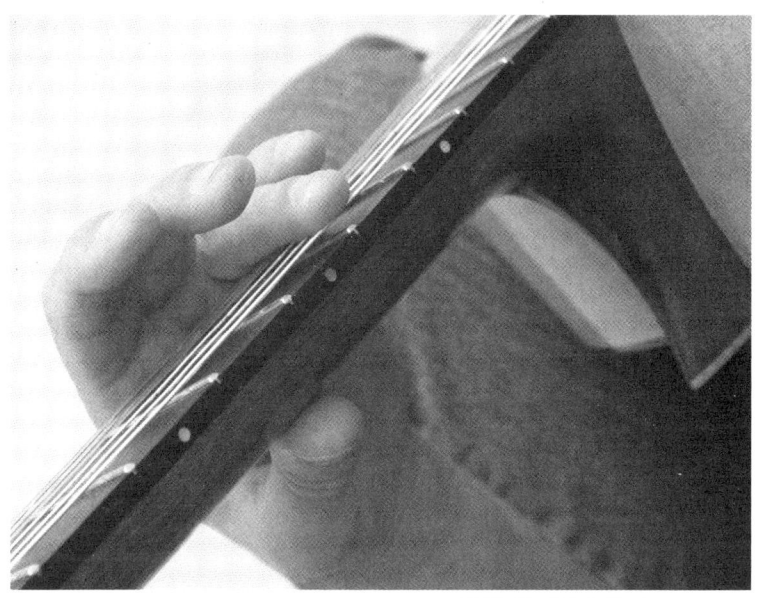

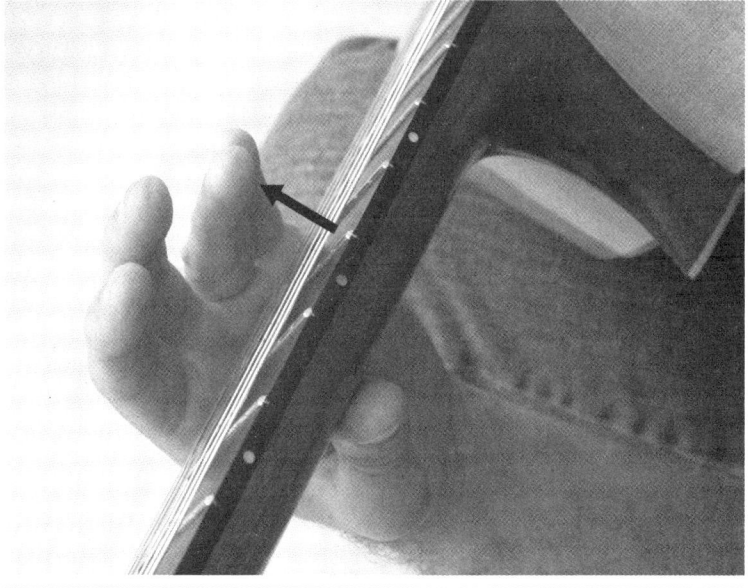

Above: Figure No. 26
Center: Figure No. 27
Below: Figure No. 28

ARTIFICIAL HARMONICS

Artificial harmonics are produced by finding the octave of a given note (which is fretted with the left hand) and using the right hand to both touch the string lightly at that point and to pluck the string. The index finger of the right hand is used to touch the string exactly as a left hand finger does when producing natural harmonics, using as little surface area as possible. The right hand also plucks the string, using either the anular finger or the thumb, depending on the desired sound; as much stretch as possible must be kept between the index finger and the plucking finger (see *Figures Nos. 29-31*).

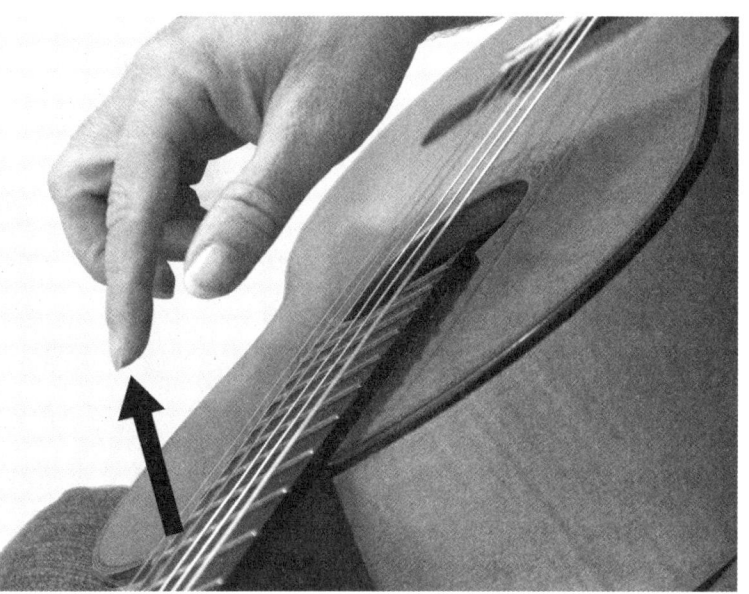

Above: Figure No. 29
Center: Figure No. 30
Below: Figure No. 31

Like the Right-Hand Studies, above, these Left-Hand Studies are drawn from Mauro Giuliani's Op. 1 (1812). I have omitted all of the composer's fingerings from these exercises so that students will use as many different fingerings as they are able to devise. These exercises should be part of every guitarist's daily practice.

Giuliani Left-Hand Studies

Giuliani Left Hand Studies

Mauro Giuliani

57

4

6

8

63

10

12

15

71

The father of modern guitar technique, Francisco Tárrega.

Gymnastic Exercises

Most of the following exercises were the warm-up exercises of Francisco Tárrega, as taught to my father by Daniel Fortea. I have added several original exercises to this group. I perform these exercises every morning.

It was my father's belief and practice that a guitarist should have a daily routine of technical exercises through which he can check every aspect of the mechanics of playing and then, immediately after doing so, spend time playing through selected repertoire. Because the exercises reinforce the technical and mechanical aspects of playing, you may then give free rein to your musical sensibilities when playing the repertoire, and free yourself of any thought of technique while performing. These pieces—the exercises and the repertoire—become lifelong companions.

Exercises Nos. 1-2 are for the left hand only. The reason for gently holding down the fingers that are not playing is to isolate all movement to a single finger, to develop independence. The velocity and force of the hammers and pull-offs should be the same with all fingers.

In **Exercise No. 3**, the fingers that are not playing hover just above the string, minimizing unneccessary movement. Continue to the ninth fret and return to the first.

In **Exercises Nos. 4-7**, repeat the pattern at each fret up to IX, then return, one fret at a time, to the first fret.

In **Exercise No. 8**, hold down the *barré* at the fret indicated, as if to play a chord, and also hold down fingers 2, 3, and 4 as shown. Move only the single fingers in the sequence. Repeat the pattern up the neck to X, and then return to the first fret.

Exercise No. 9, the "Walking Exercise," should be played without rocking the left hand. Continue to XII and return to the first fret on each string.

Exercise No. 10 is a true chromatc scale. Repeat the pattern on all strings; on the first string, continue to XIX as shown. **Exercise No. 11** is a variant of the chromatic scale; repeat the pattern on all strings. On the first string, continue to fret XIX.

Exercise No. 12 should also be repeated on all six strings; on the first string, go up to fret XIX. Be sure to minimize the movements of the left-hand fingers.

Exercises Nos. 13-15 are crossing exercises. Repeat **Exercise No. 13** on strings ② & ③, ③ & ④, ④ & ⑤, and ⑤ & ⑥. In **Exercise No. 14**, the "Spider," when the fingers release their position, they immediately hover over their next position.

Left-Hand Only Exercise: Hammers and Pull-offs. Dampen strings with right hand; the velocity and force of the hammers and pull-offs should be the same with all fingers.

1

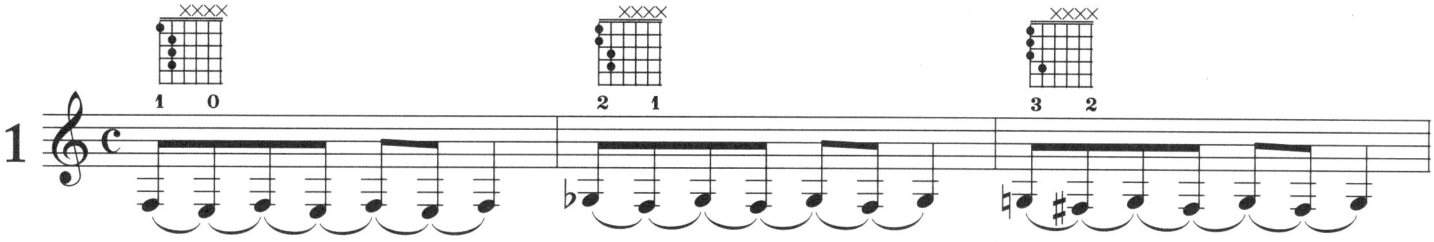

Hold, but do not play, left-hand fingers 2, 3, and 4 on the fifth string

Hold, but do not play, left-hand fingers 1, 3, and 4 as shown.

Hold, but do not play, left-hand fingers 1, 2, and 4 as shown.

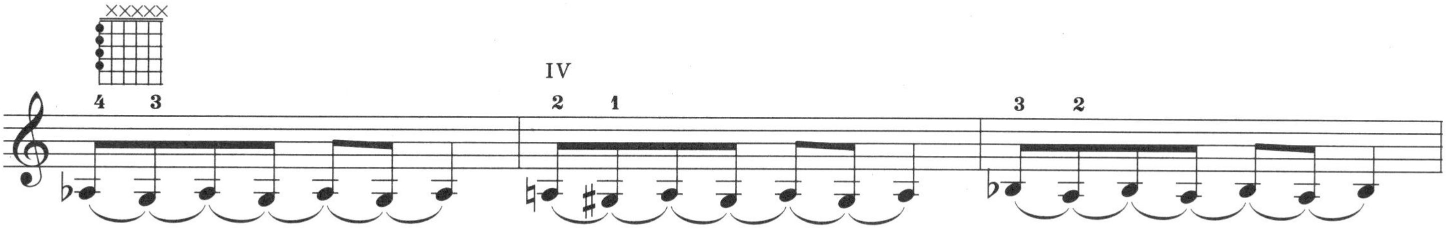

Hold, but do not play, left-hand fingers 1, 2, and 3 as shown.

Shift to IVth position and Continue the same pattern

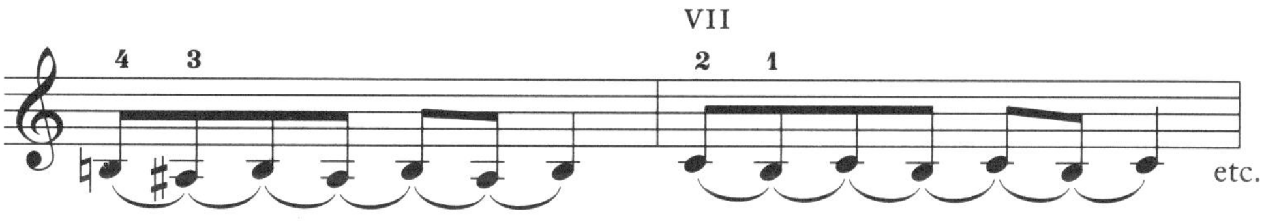

Shift to VIIth position and Continue the same pattern

Repeat on ⑤, ④, ③, ② etc.

On ①, no other fingers are held down.

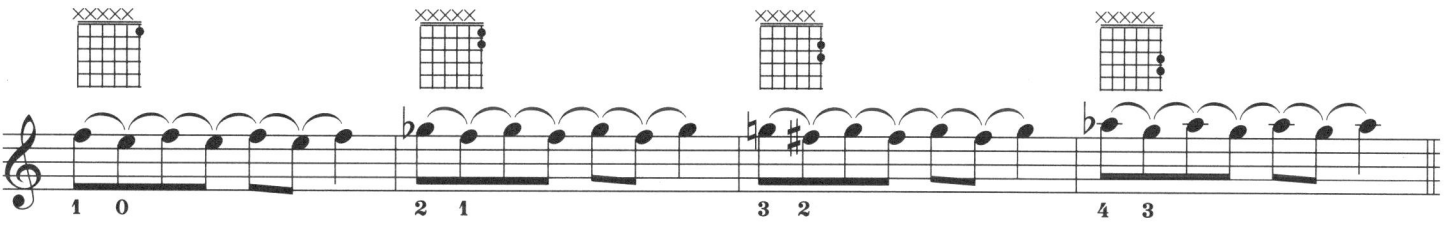

Left-Hand Only Exercise
Dampen strings with right hand; the velocity and force of the hammers and pull-offs should be the same with all fingers.

Continue to the ninth fret and return to the first fret on each string

When 1, 2, and 4 play, 3 hovers just above the string.　　　　　　　　　　When 1, 3, and 4 play, 2 hovers just above the string.

Continue to the ninth fret and return to the first fret on each string

Continue to the ninth fret and return to the first fret on each string

5

Continue pattern, descending to F♮on ⑥

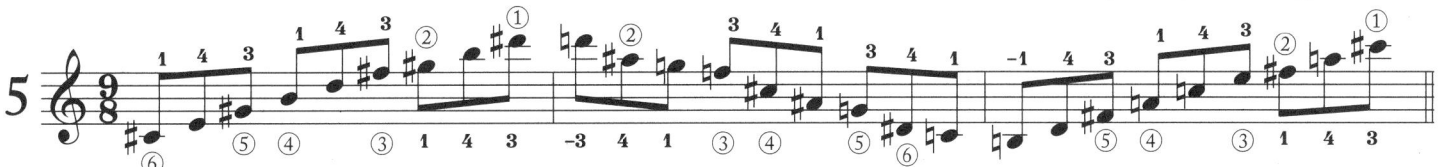

Continue to the ninth fret and return to the first fret on each string

6

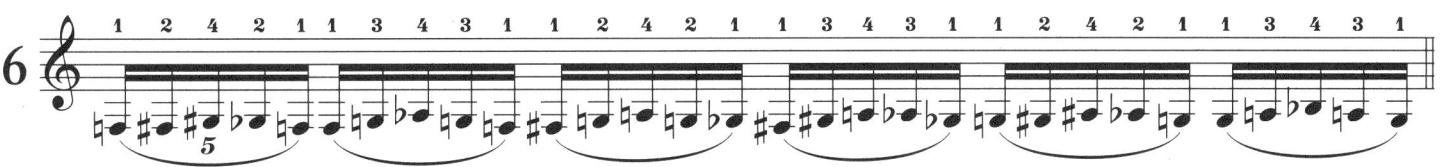

Continue to the ninth fret and return to the first fret on each string

7

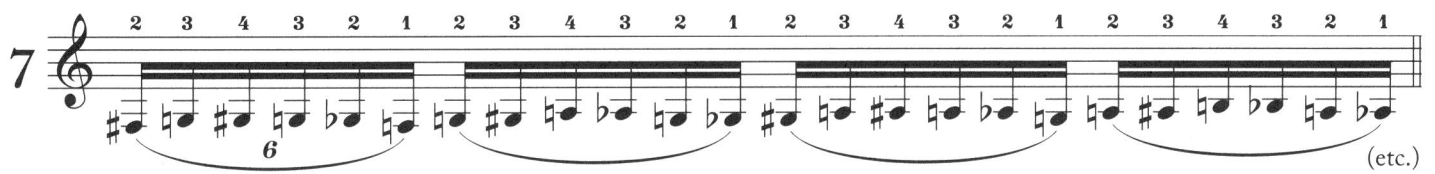

(etc.)

Continue to the tenth fret and return to the second fret on each string

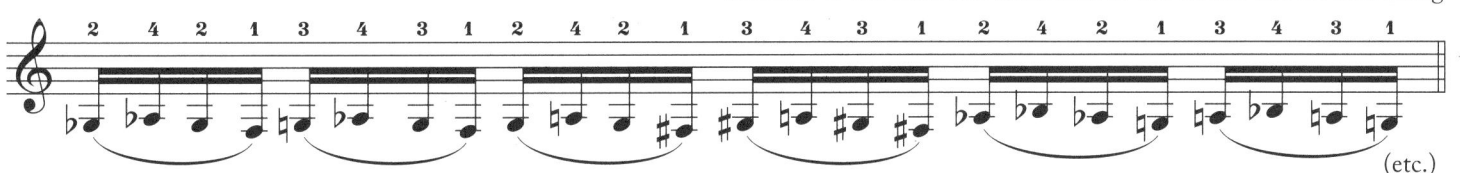

(etc.)

8

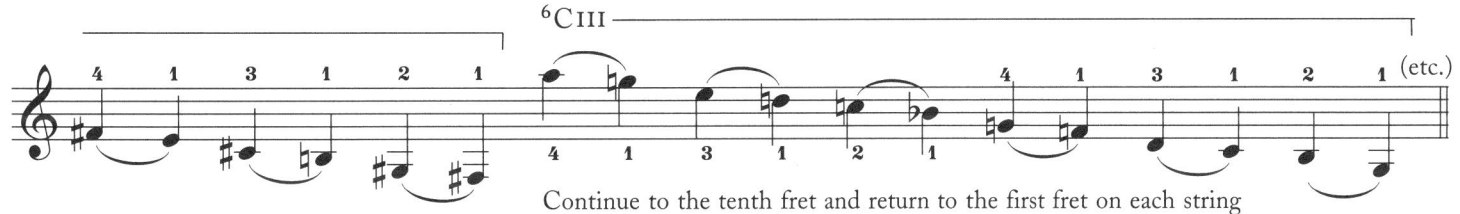

(etc.)

Continue to the tenth fret and return to the first fret on each string

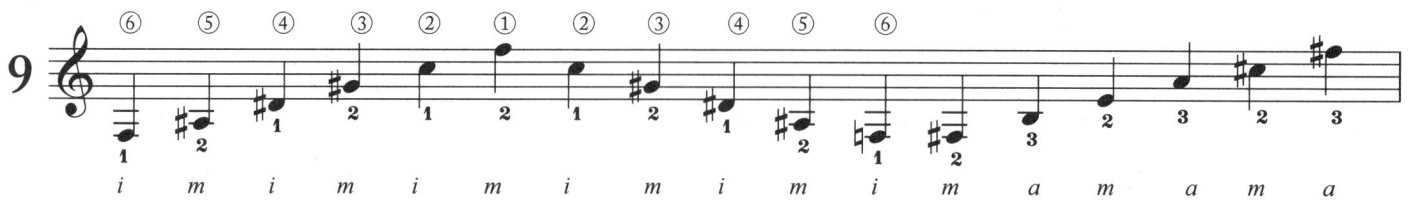

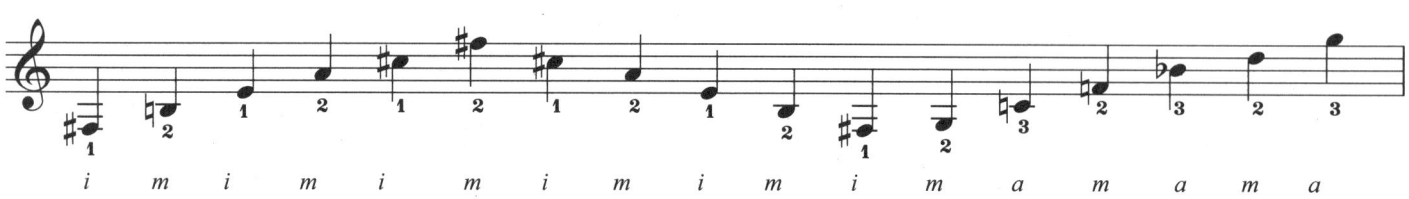

Continue to the twelfth fret and return to the first fret on each string

10

Repeat pattern on ⑤, ④, ③, ②

On ① continue to the XIXth fret.

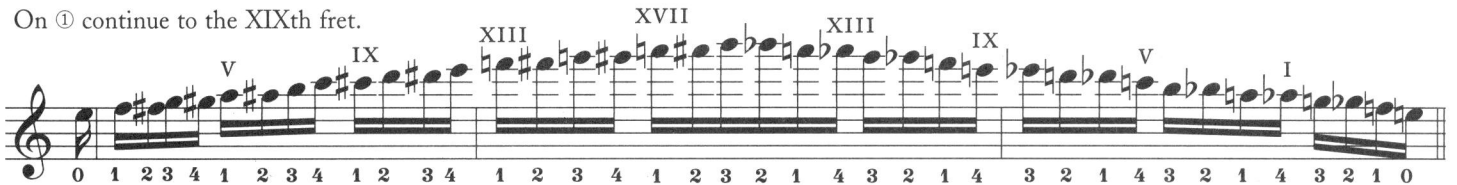

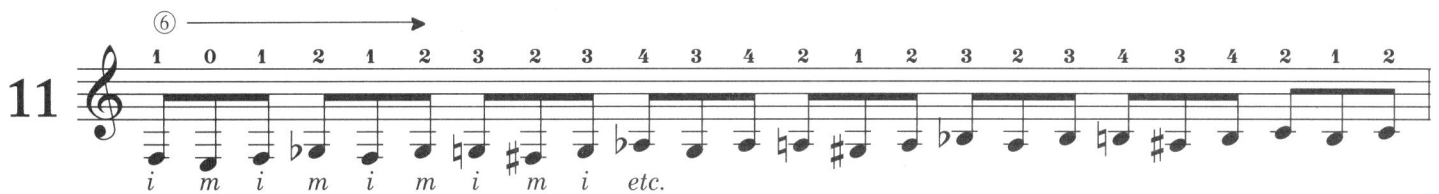

11

i   m   i   m   i   m   i   m   i   etc.

Repeat the same pattern on all other strings; on the first string, one may continue up to the 19th fret.

79

Continue on to the 13th fret on all strings;
advanced players continue to the 19th fret on the first string

Repeat the pattern
on all strings

Above: Pepe Romero at the Court of the Lions in the Alhambra, Granada.
Below: The Romero family at the Alhambra, c. 1948, from left: Unidentified, Salvador
Gallego (Pepe's grandfather), Celín, Celedonio, Pepe, Angelita, Angel, Juana Muñoz.

Tremolo

*T*remolo is a technical device that gives the guitar the capability to play the long, sustained notes of bowed or stringed instruments. Tremolo has two aspects, the bass line played by the thumb, and the melody, usually played by *a–m–i*. The repeated pattern should be felt and heard as one continuous sound.

The bass opens up and maintains the space in which the tremolo exists. The cycle should be understood as *a–m–i–p* rather than *p–a–m–i*. For example, when we begin to play *Recuerdos de la Alhambra*, the first thumb stroke serves to open the space into which the tremolo flows:

p, a–m–i–p, a–m–i–p, a–m–i–p, a–m–i–p, etc.

so that the *a* finger is the singer of the melody, and the *m–i* sustains the note created by *a*. The thumb, which is playing the beat, is the resolution of the cycle, not the beginning. In all music, we anticipate, we look forward to the beat, which resolves the rhythm. The beat should be felt not as a point of departure but as a destination, as in this example by Bach.

Courante (J. S. Bach)

As has been noted earlier, it is very important that at any given instant in the pattern, each finger is at a different point in its orbit: one is in flight during its follow-through, another is returning to find the string to be played next, and the other is touching the string being played.

Flamenco players usually use a five-note tremolo which is performed *p–i–a–m–i*. The same general principles apply to performing the Flamenco tremolo, but the *i* finger has a different rhythmic sequence, providing a syncopated feeling without affecting the evenness of the five notes.

p   i   a   m   i   p   i   a   m   i   p   i   a   m   i   p

Improvisación: ¡A Granada! Cantiga Árabe

Málaga, 8 octobre 1899

(Recuerdos de la Alhambra)

Edited by Pepe Romero

Francisco Tárrega

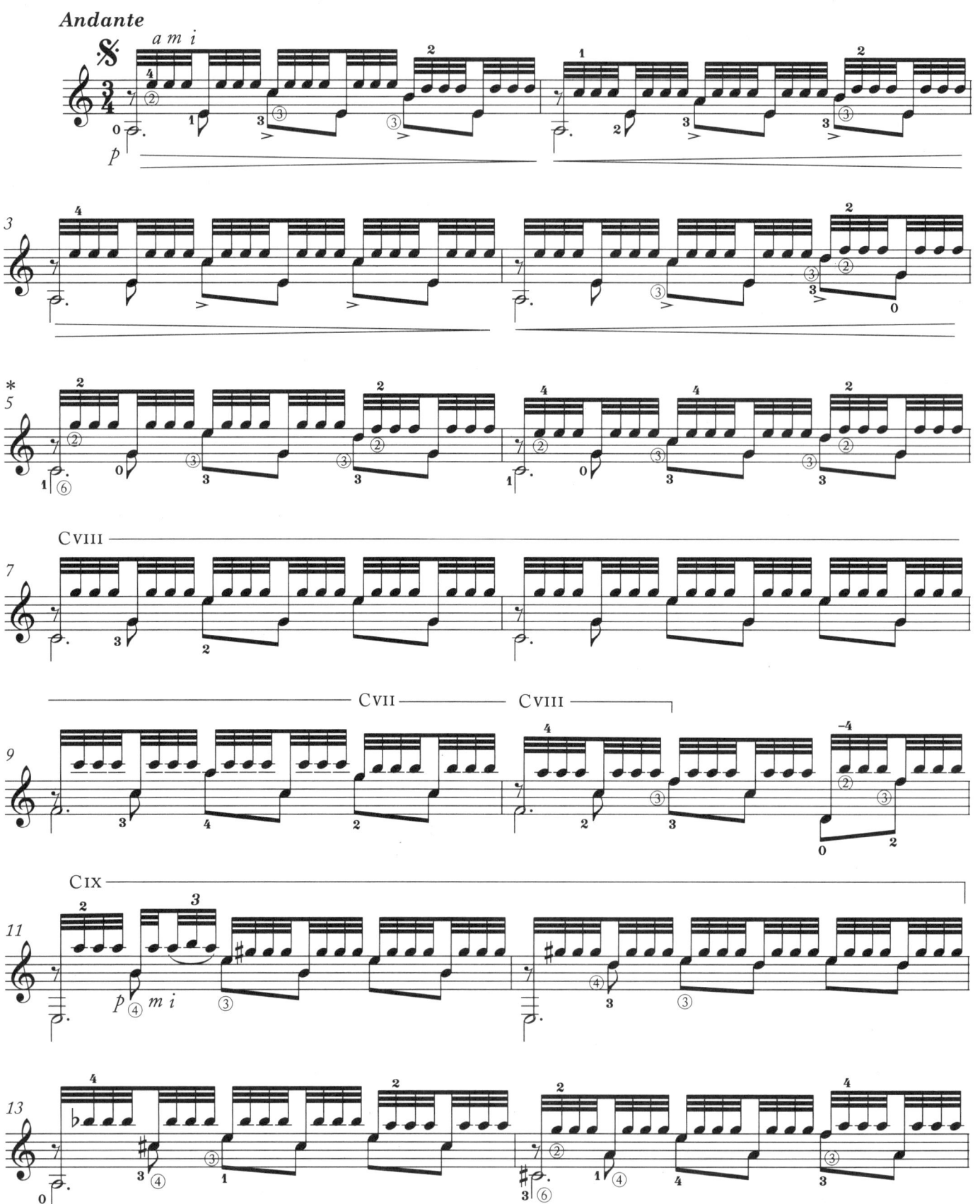

* In a manuscript from Málaga dated October 8, 1899, Tárrega plays this section with a barré III.
The fingering provided here is the way I play the piece.

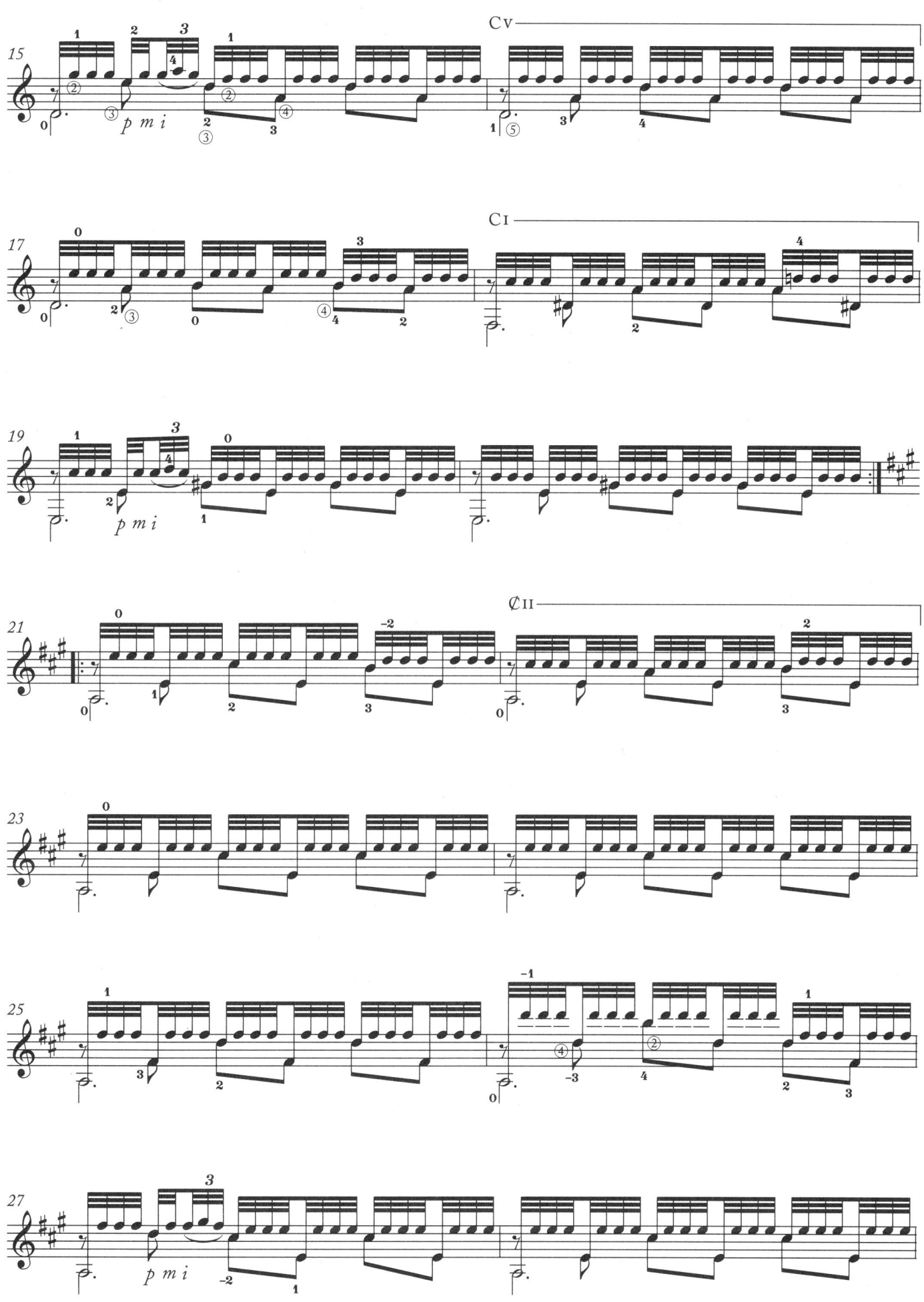

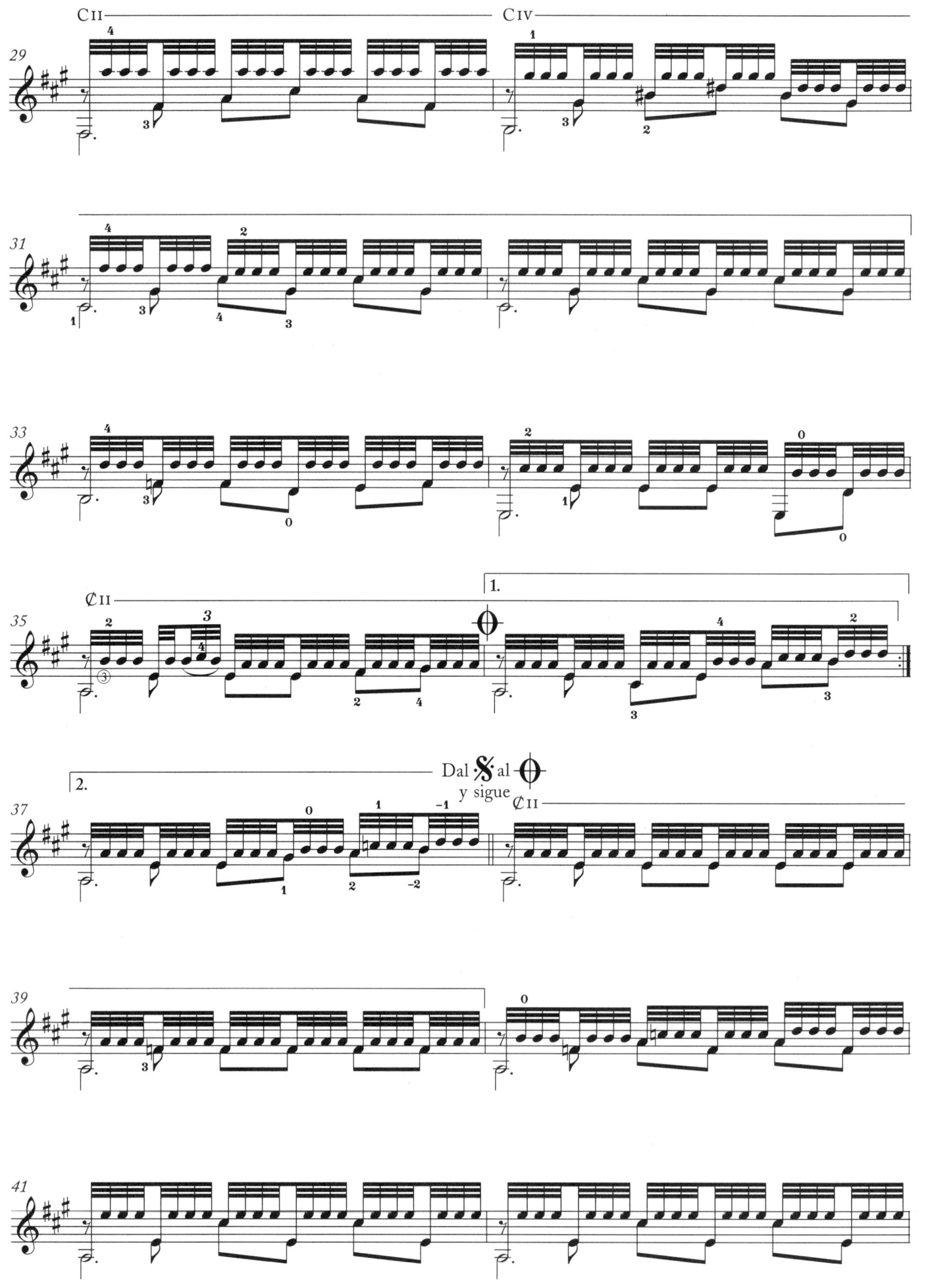

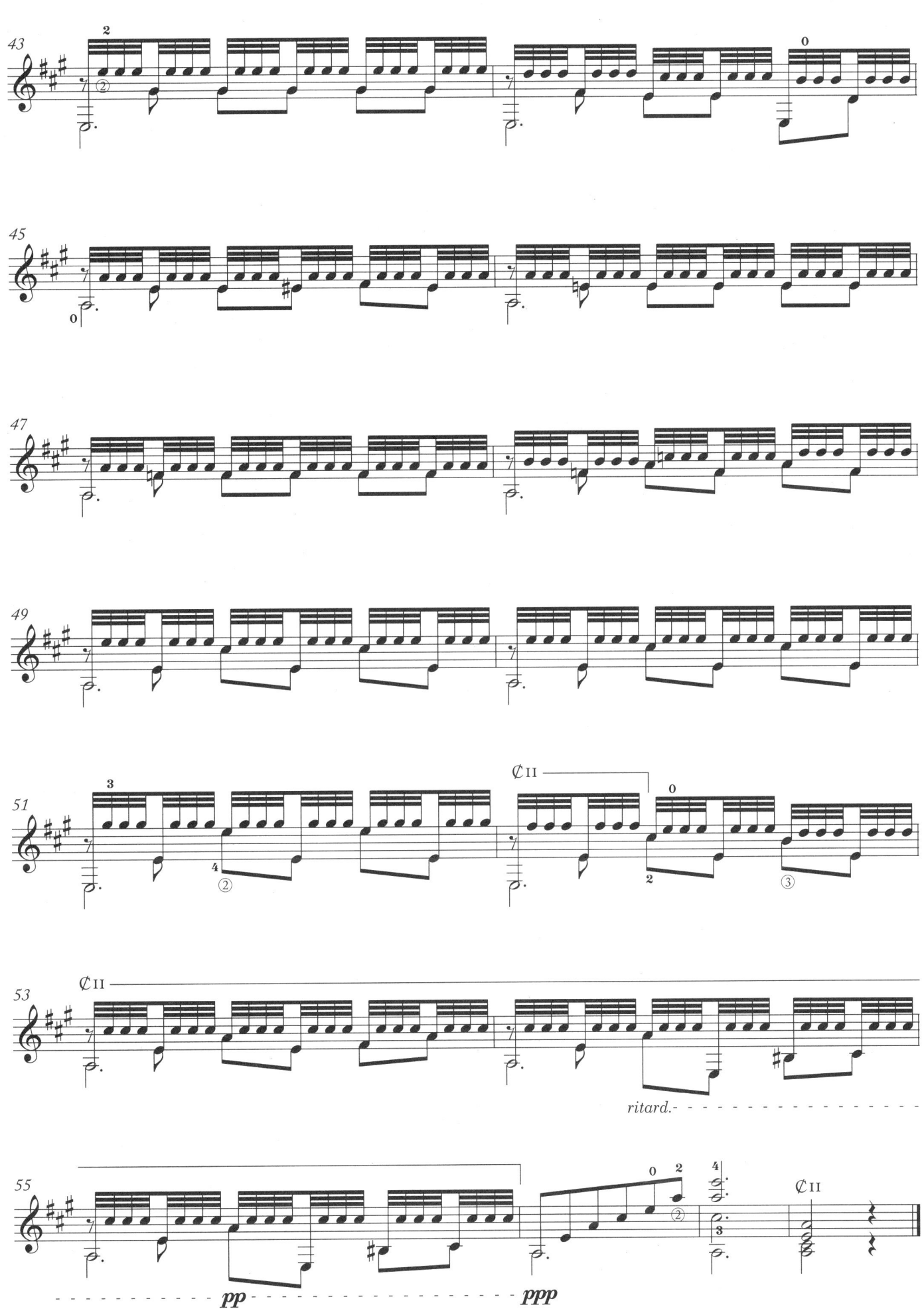

89

Juerga, a drawing by Pepe Romero, 1962

Flamenco

*I*t is my intention and purpose in writing this book to share with my disciples all of my training and technique. It, therefore, must include some flamenco techniques and a traditional flamenco dance.

Flamenco has had a major role in the inspiration of all the Spanish composers who have written so well for our instrument. It has also had a large part in the formation of the Spanish school of guitar playing.

I have chosen the traditional form of *alegrías* (which is one of the most popular dances in flamenco) for its rhythmic drive and its effectiveness as a right-hand study.

The *alegrías* consists of phrases of twelve beats, with the accents falling on the third, sixth, eighth, tenth, and twelfth. It is normally written in four measures of triple time (see *Figure No. 31*). I have chosen, however, to write it alternating two measures of triple time with three measures of duple, making the accents always fall on the downbeat (see *Figure No. 32*).

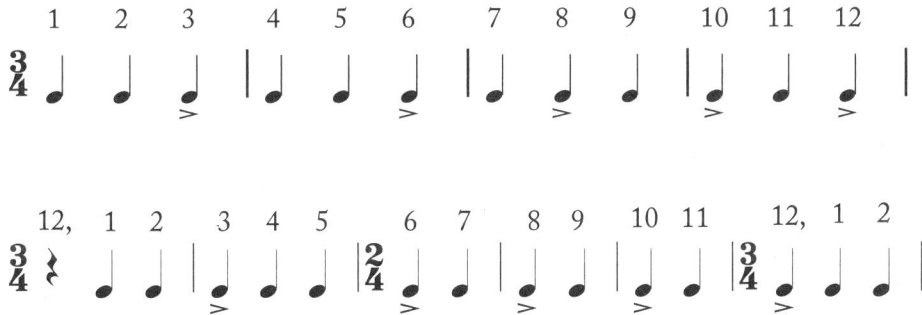

Figures No. 31 (above) and 32 (below)

The only flamenco techniques I have used that are different from those previously discussed are various forms of *rasgueados* (strumming with the back side of the nails).

Daily practice of this technique has been proven to dramatically increase a player's speed in scales, arpeggios, and tremolos.

Rasgueado

I have notated the direction in which the finger strums by the following signs on the top of the designated chords:

⊓ —ascending strum, from the bass to the treble

∨ —descending strum, from the treble to the bass

When there is a sign at the beginning of a group or a series of strokes, the direction

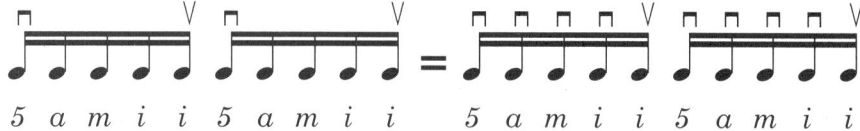

5 a m i i 5 a m i i   5 a m i i 5 a m i i

does not change until a new sign indicates the change. In order to notate fingerings in the *rasgueados*, I have marked the little finger of the right hand with the number "5."

Keep the 5, *a*, and *m* extended and play back and forth with the *i*.

i   i   i   i   i   i

Play the ascending stroke with the *a*, *m* and *i* fingers simultaneously and use only the *i* finger on the descending stroke; then return the a and *m* fingers together to position without hitting the strings. This technique is used for accents.

a   i   a   i   a   i
m   m   m
i   i   i

Make a fist and play each ascending stroke by extending each finger with as much velocity as possible. Use the descending *i* finger to return the 5, *a*, and *m* fingers to their starting positions, although only *i* strokes the strings.

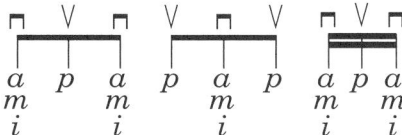

This technique is done by keeping the wrist very straight and rotating the arm from the elbow. Start with the fingers in a fist. As they play the ascending strokes, they extend; on the thumbs descending strokes they contract, closing the hand.

The sequence of photographs on the preceding page and this page illustrate the above rasgueado.

Keep the wrist straight and rotate the arm at the elbow. The fingers and thumb play very much as in Number 4 (above), but with the addition of the fifth finger and the fingers extending independently.

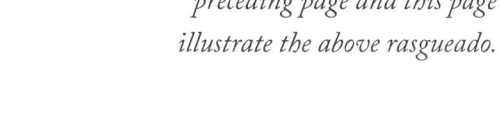

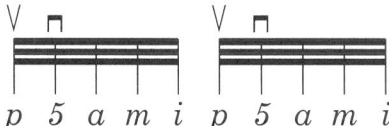

Alegrías

Pepe Romero

95

Tempo primo

96

Celedonio Romero
Estudios and Compositions

Celedonio Romero, painted by Pepe Romero.

Celedonio Romero, painted by Larry Kastner.

The following seven studies and five solo pieces by my father were written for the purpose of teaching every aspect of technique to my brothers and me. These pieces are not only marvelous for building technique but also for maintaining and improving it.

Nana

This lullaby was written for me when I was born. —P.R.

Celedonio Romero

Estudio No. 1: La Mariposa

Celedonio Romero

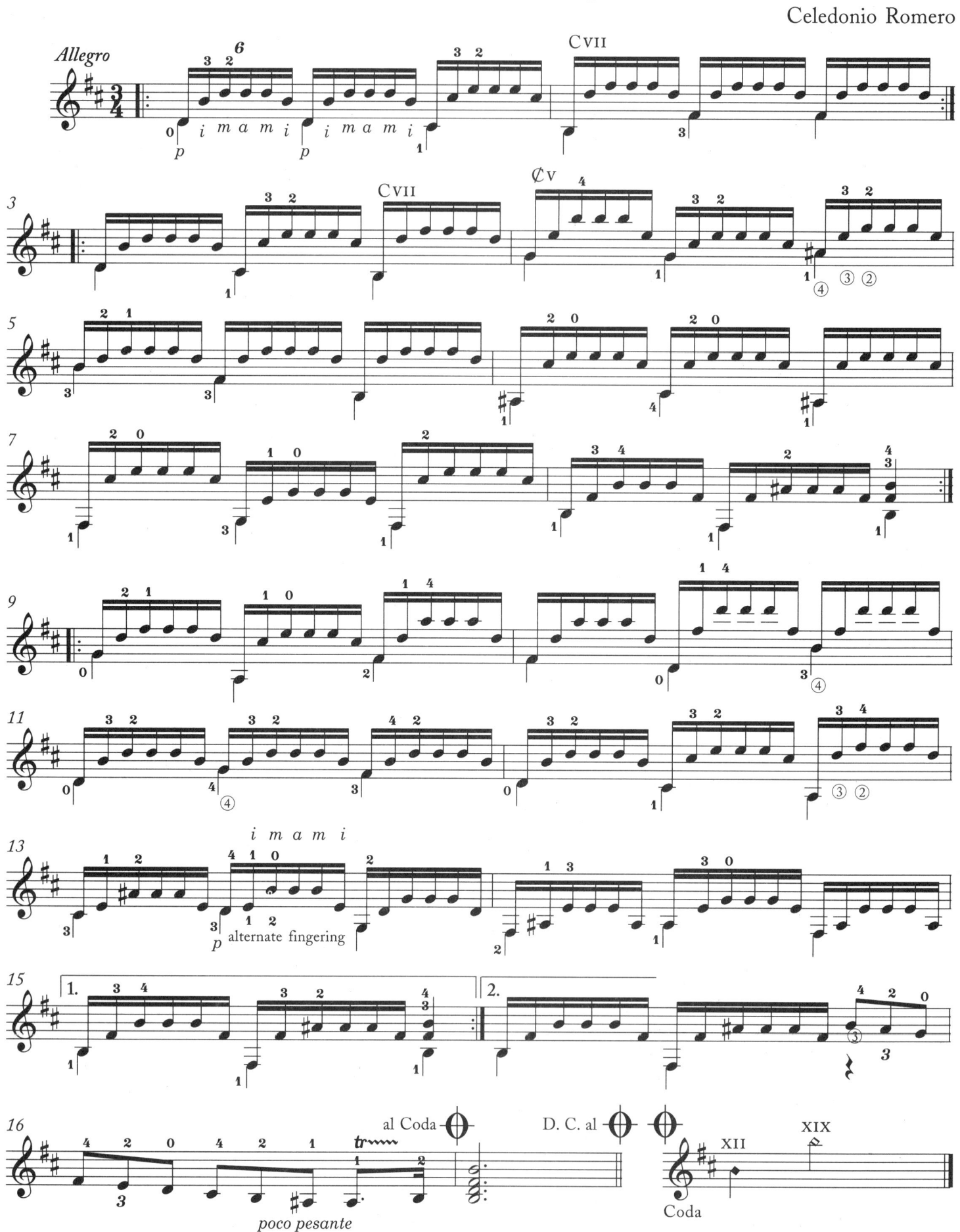

Estudio No. 2

Estudio No. 3: La Abeja

accelerando

105

Estudio No. 4

Preludio granadino (Variaciones)

Cadenza

a piacere

Allegro andante

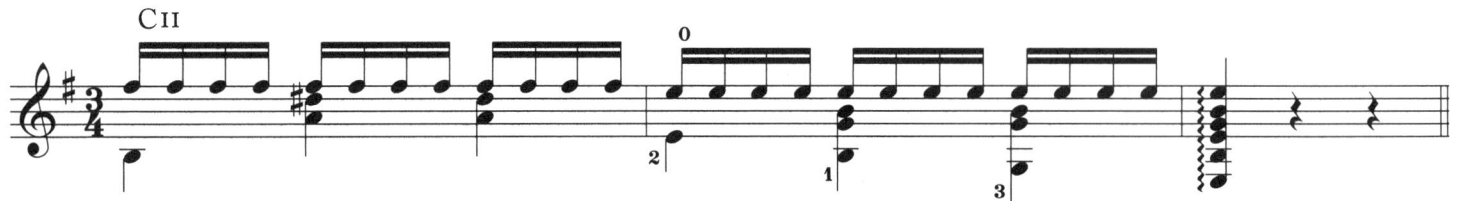

108

Estudio No. 5: Preludio

Estudio No. 6: El Gaditano (Preludio)

113

Estudio No. 7: Estudio de concierto

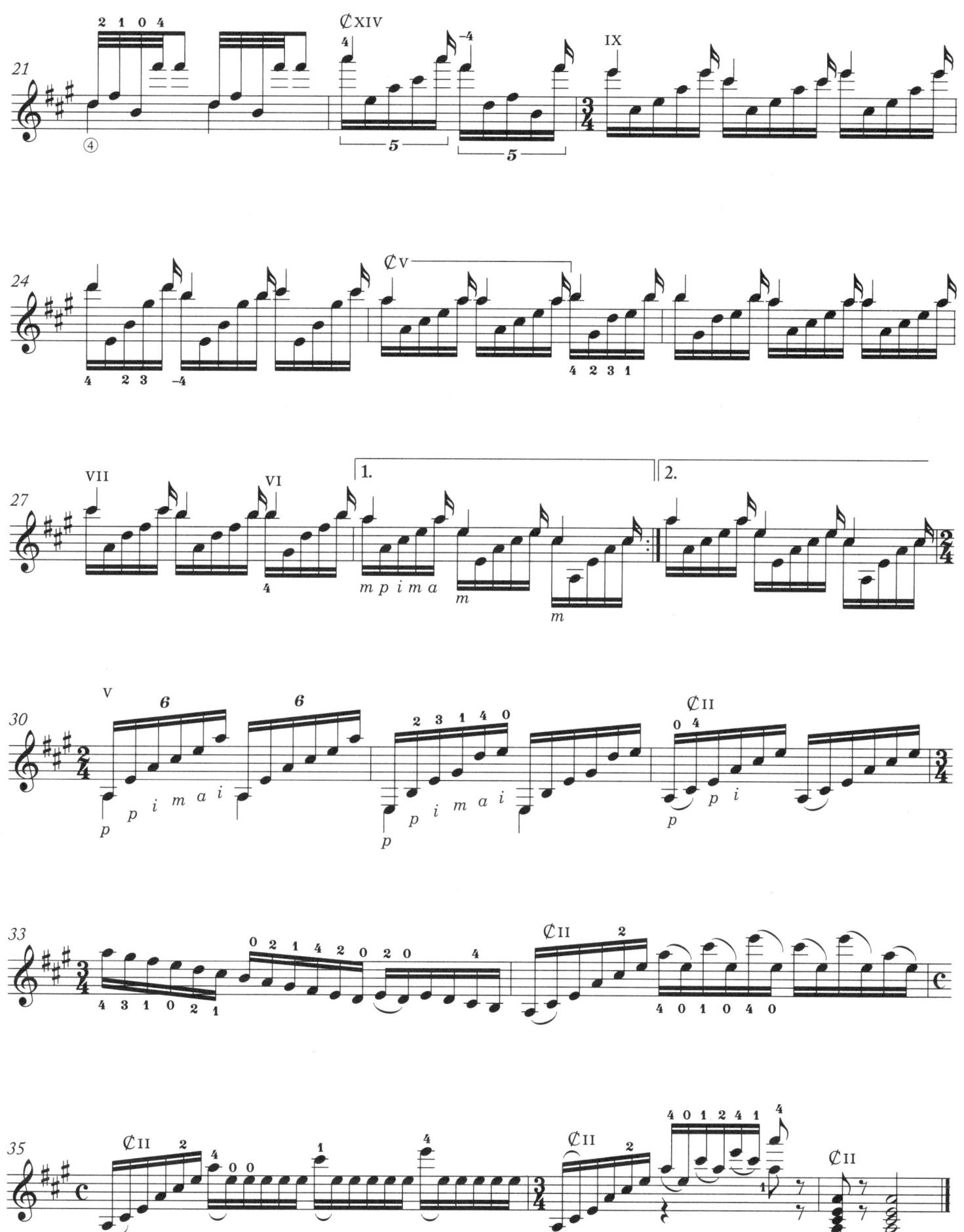

115

Canción al alba No. 1

Canción al alba No. 2

119

Oración

The Concert Artist

The principal problem that takes place during a public performance is that the performer finds himself imprisoned by his ego, which locks his thoughts in the difficulty of the work he is to perform and in the impact that the success or failure of his performance will have upon him. This state of consciousness will make the artist uncomfortably aware of who is in the audience and what power they may be able to exert upon him.

This state of mind will escalate and multiply in negative effect if the performance is to be preserved by recording. A very prejudicial ramification of this state of mind is to compare ourselves with our colleagues and to think that we have to maintain or surpass an established level of performance that we think exists in the minds of the public or the critics, or in our own minds.

Music has nothing to do with any of these thoughts. Music is abstract, spiritual, and sensual. It is fantastic dreams that fly in the heights of infinity, transcending time and space. In order to be transported by music, we must conquer the ego and stop negative thoughts before they take place. The interpreter or concert artist must recreate and give life to the work that was created by the composer and which then lies dormant inside musical symbols on paper—symbols that represent the most profound and secret sentiments of the composer.

The performer has to read the work totally free from preconceived thoughts; he must unite his own thoughts and sentiments with those of the composer in the same way that, when reading a novel, one joins the characters and circumstances in it. The musical sounds have reality, colors, forms, and shapes, and—above all—an infinity of personality and character. In music we must find mountains, valleys, rivers, oceans, little flowers and big forests, the knowledge of wise men and the innocence of children, the peaceful and profound love for God and the passionate love between a man and a woman, the love of parents, siblings, and children … love in all of its manifestations. It must have darkness and it must have light; it must have storms and it must have peace. In the great works of music, the whole of creation is written.

To unite with the spirit of the composer, we must think with the subconscious and not the conscious part of the mind, thus opening the door and entering the castle of fantasy that exists in the depths of each of us. In order to achieve this, we must learn to give the conscious mind and the subconscious mind their proper respective tasks.

When a piece of music has made a mark in our heart and soul, we must decide if it is to be incorporated into our repertory. The ego will ask us if the piece will serve to demonstrate our technical facility. If we permit ourselves even the most minimal contemplation of this theme, we can be certain that any degree of energy spent in this consideration will be manifested and multiplied in the form of nerves and doubts when the piece is performed in front of an audience. The question we should ask ourselves, instead, is whether we have the adequate and correct qualifications to perform the work as the composer intended. If the decision is positive, the energy we spent in this reflection will also be manifested at the moment we find ourselves in front of an audience, but in this case, the consequences will be peaceful and positive. In the words of the great composer Giuseppe Verdi, "Music is not to impress others but to move them."

Virtuosity is a gift, much like any other gift such as health, fortune, or beauty. The artist who finds himself in possession of this gift of virtuosity has great responsibility but also must face certain dangers. He has the responsibility to cultivate and maintain his gift in the service of music and for those who wish and need to hear this music. He also has the duty to teach and transmit this knowledge of his art without reservation to young artists so they may build and develop their own abilities. The principal danger is to give free rein to the ego, to use the gift to rejoice vainly in a feeling of superiority over others. The consequences of this will, at some point, be devastating and can reduce a great artist into a miserable individual, blinded by the veil of nerves and jealousy, incapable of partaking in the pure joy of music.

After selecting the piece of music, the interpreter must put his mechanics to the test. First, he must find a fingering that perfectly merges the technical demands of the work and the physical capacities of the interpreter. Through the fingering, he must overcome all obsacles that may get in the way of the piece singing freely.

Once the fingering has been determined, we enter the next stage, committing the piece to memory through repetition until developing what my father called *automatismo*. By this, I mean that we play without conscious thought of the movements of the hands. This is also called tactual memory, and is a crucial state to achieve before a public performance. Once we have achieved it, we must never doubt or question the ability of our hands to perform.

To achieve *automatismo*, we must make many repetitions, visualizing the position of each note on the fingerboard with the conscious part of the mind aware of the movements of both hands, assigning to each note the same importance, and always incorporating dynamics, no matter how slowly we are practicing.

For every sound there exists a corresponding physical sensation. One must maintain a continual relationship among the sensations, the movements, and the sounds. This relationship must be reinforced by practice at reduced speeds. No matter how well we know a piece, we must repeat it frequently to reduce those accidents that can occur during a public performance. The repetitions can be practiced with and without the instrument. I must clarify that this practice is only for the visual and the tactual memory, so that it may be possible that, at the time of peformance, we reverse the process and allow the subconscious mind to take over.

One starts by hearing the appropriate sound inside the mind and, while the body recalls the physical sensation of the sound, the hands automatically go to the necessary places and make the necessary movements. Thus, the sound in the mind of the performer can be reproduced. From the beginning of the preparation, we must study the æsthetic and sonorous concept of the piece, giving dimension and perspective to the dynamics of the musical lines so that they can be, from the start, absorbed by the subconscious mind.

While acquiring the mechanical *automatismo*, but not at the same time, we must work the mind without the instrument, singing and listening to the piece inside our thoughts. Such mental exercises should not be limited to music we are learning or playing, but also to music for other instruments, for voice, as well as chamber and symphonic music. If we practice this daily, we can achieve the ability to hear music in our imagination and thoughts with the vividness of a live or recorded perfomance. Once we have acquired the mechanical *automatismo*, it will be merged with our sonorous thoughts and the voice of the instrument itself.

The eyes also play an important role in choreographing the movements of the hands, but we must let the hands work independently; the eyes are observers, not directors, of the movements and positions of the hands. Remember that this is after we have achieved the mechanical *automatismo*.

The ears serve to coordinate the sound that comes from the instrument with the music in the mind of the performer, resulting in a perfectly focused synchronization of the interior and the exterior. Before playing a piece, connect to the silence. A piece must have an empty space into which it emerges.

Automatismo

We must re-create the feeling of deep sleep and, just like a dream, the music fills the empty space we have created for it.

Before we bring a work to the stage, we must be convinced that we have done everything in our power to give it the correct preparation, so that we may say, "I am prepared and ready to receive whatever result the performance may have."

It is useful to visualize the concert by mentally simulating the total experience. We can start by selecting an imaginary place—a theater or hall—where the artist wishes to perform. While bathing and preparing just as if the concert was taking place, we think about the program to be played and the effect the music has upon us. It is good practice to sing the pieces in the program. Dressed and ready to face the imaginary public, we picture ourselves in the dressing room. It is of great importance to avoid dehydration or lowered blood sugar levels, and I always have something to drink, either water or fruit juice, and some fruit (bananas in particular seem to have a tranquillizing effect upon the nervous system).

The warming of the hands should be gradual, beginning with some chromatic and diatonic scales, and progressing to selected studies for both hands such as those of Mauro Giuliani and the gymnastic exercises from this book. We then play through one or two of our favorite studies.

Having prepared the hands, we must recheck the tuning of the guitar as precisely as possible. Some moments alone with closed eyes, taking long and slow breaths, contemplating how inhaling bathes the body with energy, and exhaling carries away impurities.

Finally, we must walk to the stage with security, peace, and faith. After taking a seat and reviewing the tuning, take a deep and peaceful breath and begin the concert. Before playing each piece, have the rhythm pulsating within. Feel several measures of rhythm before beginning, and never lose this awareness of the pulse as you play. Rhythm is like a fountain of energy for the performer. It will keep the structure together and the undulation helps dissolve nervousness. Rhythm is hypnotic. Once set in motion, it becomes its own entity; one rises it like a wave. While playing, the artist should constantly sing the music in his mind, and enjoy the concert as a listener rather than trying to direct it. Let the music assume its own shape, passing freely through the mind and body, bathing the ears with its powerful and purifying magic. When we find ourselves in an actual concert, we must do exactly as in the simulation above, but we will find an important difference. A real audience creates a great energy that grows and multiplies with each additional member. This is positive energy and of great value to the artist, who must learn to receive it, to merge it with his own. This energy facilitates the artist's ability to enter a state of superconsciousness, and the concert becomes what the pianist Artur Rubinstein called "moments of the infinite."

Celedonio Romero, by Baldomero Romero Ressendi

Developing Vibratory Sense

*M*usic is received through our sensory input, primarily auditory and vibratory. When merging these two—auditory and vibratory—we open ourselves to the awareness of emotions and we enter a dreamlike state in which the power of creativity can take over and the visual sense joins in stimulating fantastic images. Being in this state opens up the fountain of love that is the core of our beings and allows us to become the very music we are playing, creating a magic circle in which playing the music and being played by it are one and the same things.

To work on developing the vibratory sense:

1. Close your eyes and hold your guitar in such a way that you feel merged with it into a single corporeal entity, an embrace that creates the musical being that is the guitarist.

2. Become aware of each of the contact points between yourself and the guitar.

3. Play a note and feel how the guitar vibrates at each contact point.

4. Concentrate on one point at a time, later merging them together. First feel how the guitar vibrates and then how the vibration has penetrated your body through the Merkel cells in the skin, the neuro-endocrine receptor cells, developing a full-body vibratory sense.

5. Start playing low notes, taking time to feel them. Later, play scales, arpeggios, and eventually complete pieces.

Through this practice, you will awaken pleasure centers that will help to guide you through the music-making process.

The Metaphysics of Music

*M*usic is a universe unto itself, a cosmos consisting of the performers, the instruments, the composers, the instrument makers, and the audience (because listening, too, is an art).

Music necessarily emerges from silence, from the great void, via the same dialectical process that governs all existence. This is the nature of music, the nature of life, the journey of silence, the birth of death. When we play or create or feel a piece of music, we duplicate the cosmic process of creation—all creation begins with nothing.

Music develops a consciousness of the moment with an awareness of infinity. When experiencing music, one feels the past, the present, and the future brought together in the moment.

Music is sound organized by time (rhythm). Both time and silence are infinite. Just as silence is infinite, so too is sound, but our awareness of it is measured by rhythm / time. Sound is the alteration of silence; rhythm is the alteration of time. Sound requires, satisfies, and fulfills silence, and vice-versa.

Rhythm is energy. It is related to the sources and manifestations of life itself: breath, pulse, magnetism, gravity, the tides. While all rhythms may be comprehended in groups of two or three, they are ultimately part of a single entity, the musical piece in question.

Music enables us to commune with the universe and our own spiritual natures. Music is a divine gift from the creator of all things that, with it and through it, we can find both our humanity and our immortality.

*E*verything I have written in this book must be learned through your conscious mind and should be reviewed frequently throughout your career as a guitarist. All of it is usable, however, only when controlled and directed exclusively by your subconscious mind.

Prior to performing, you should consciously slow your breathing, inhaling and exhaling to a comfortable count. Taking deep rhythmical breaths, empty your mind of any disturbing thoughts; at the same time relax from your feet to your neck, paying careful attention to each and every part of your body.

(It is especially important that your calves, thighs, buttocks, abdomen, and shoulders be relaxed when you play.) At this point you should withdraw your consciousness from your body and place it in the crown of your head; it is there that the conception of all musical sounds takes place. With your awareness always from the crown of your head, view your hands as though they were those of another player; allow your tactual memory to guide your fingers with confidence over the fretboard and strings and balance the sound that comes out of the guitar with that which you hear in your head.

I cannot end without expressing what music has meant to me. From the beginning of my life to this moment, music has consoled my aching heart in its darkest moments and lifted me up in a cloud of ecstasies when fate and destiny have smiled upon me.

When my heart has been so overwhelmed by emotions that words or thoughts become inadequate, it always has been music that came to the rescue, impregnated by love and peace. It is that love that has guided me to write this technique book in which I share with you my craft, so that you may let your inspiration fill your heart and flow freely through your fingers.

My love shall always be with you as you search for music.

—Pepe Romero

Photos

from the

Romero

Family

Album

*From Spain
to the U.S.A.*

130

Opposite page, clockwise from top left:
Angelita and Celedonio Romero;
Pepe, Celedonio, Angelita, Angel & Celín;
Celedonio Romero;
Pepe (aged three);
Angel, Angelita, Celedonio, Pepe & Celín;
Angelita & Celedonio wedding photo;
This page, clockwise from top left:
Celín on his first guitar,
Celín, Pepe, & Angel in Málaga;
Pepe in Santa Barbara;
Pepe gets breakfast in bed;
Angelita with her three sons; Pepe in Málaga;
Pepe, Angelita, Celedonio, Celín, & Angel.

Los Romeros quartet through the years: This page, top left: the original quartet (Pepe, Celedonio, Angel, Celín):
top right: in 1958 with Angelita and Farrington Stoddard; center: on a television variety show, 1961; below: in the late 1970s.
Opposite page, clockwise from top left: the second quartet, with Celino, Celín, Celedonio & Pepe;
the recent quartet (clockwise from top left: Pepe, Celín, Celino, & Lito, with Angel; the same five; the recent quartet; the same;
Center: loading the car for a concert tour.

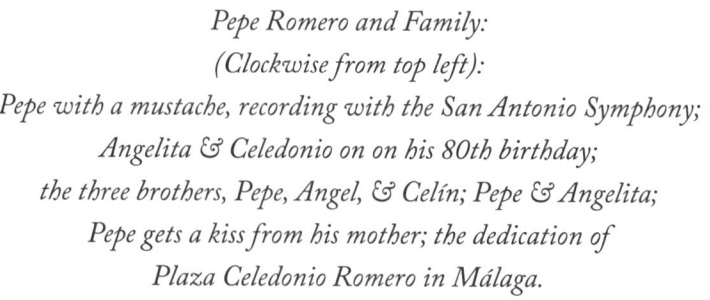

Pepe Romero and Family:
(Clockwise from top left):
Pepe with a mustache, recording with the San Antonio Symphony;
Angelita & Celedonio on on his 80th birthday;
the three brothers, Pepe, Angel, & Celín; Pepe & Angelita;
Pepe gets a kiss from his mother; the dedication of
Plaza Celedonio Romero in Málaga.

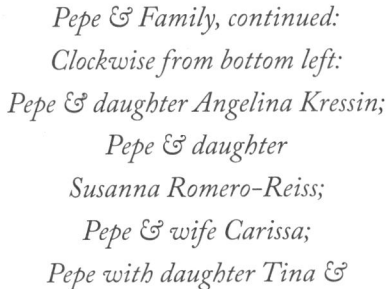

Pepe & Family, continued:
Clockwise from bottom left:
Pepe & daughter Angelina Kressin;
Pepe & daughter
Susanna Romero-Reiss;
Pepe & wife Carissa;
Pepe with daughter Tina &
son-in-law Greg Shirer; Pepe & Angelita;
Pepe & granddaughter Kristina;
Pepe & granddaughter Sophia; Pepe with
son-in-law Lane Romero-Reiss & granddaughter Kristina;
Pepe and son-in-law Joseph Kressin.
Center: Pepe's grandchildren Bernardo, Jacob, and Leah.

Pepe & Family, continued: Clockwise from above: A Romero family portrait; Pepe & Angel; Pepe & Celín; Pepe with granddaughter Leah. Center: Carissa Romero and Angelina Kressin;

Friends and Collaborators:
This page, top row: Pepe with Joaquín Rodrigo; Celedonio with Rodrigo;
second row: Pepe rehearses with Sir Neville Marriner;
Carissa Romero, Federico Moreno Torroba, his daughter Mariana, & Pepe (Madrid,
1980); Pepe with Morton Gould; third row: Pepe with Jessye Norman;
Los Romeros with Phyllis Curtin; fourth row: Pepe with Isabelle Brouwer &
Leo Brouwer; Guillermo Figueroa, Pepe, & Ernesto Cordero;
below right: Pepe and Richard Long honored by the
Guitar Foundation of America, 2011.

Friends and Collaborators: This page, clockwise from top:
Los Romeros with Jesus López-Cobos & Lorenzo Palomo;
Lorenzo Palomo with Rafael Frühbeck de Burgos;
Pepe with Gioachino Giussani; Pepe with Edi Blöchinger;
Carissa Romero with Manolo Contreras;
the brothers with Hermann Hauser II;
Pepe, Miguel Rodríguez Jr., Angel & Miguel Rodríguez Sr.
Opposite page, clockwise from top: Pepe & Philippe Entremont;
Pepe & Angel; Angel conducts Pepe;
Manolo Sanlúcar & Pepe Rodríguez with Pepe & Celín;
Los Romeros rehearse with Lorenzo Palomo (at the piano);
Pepe & Celín; Pepe & Rafael Frühbeck de Burgos.

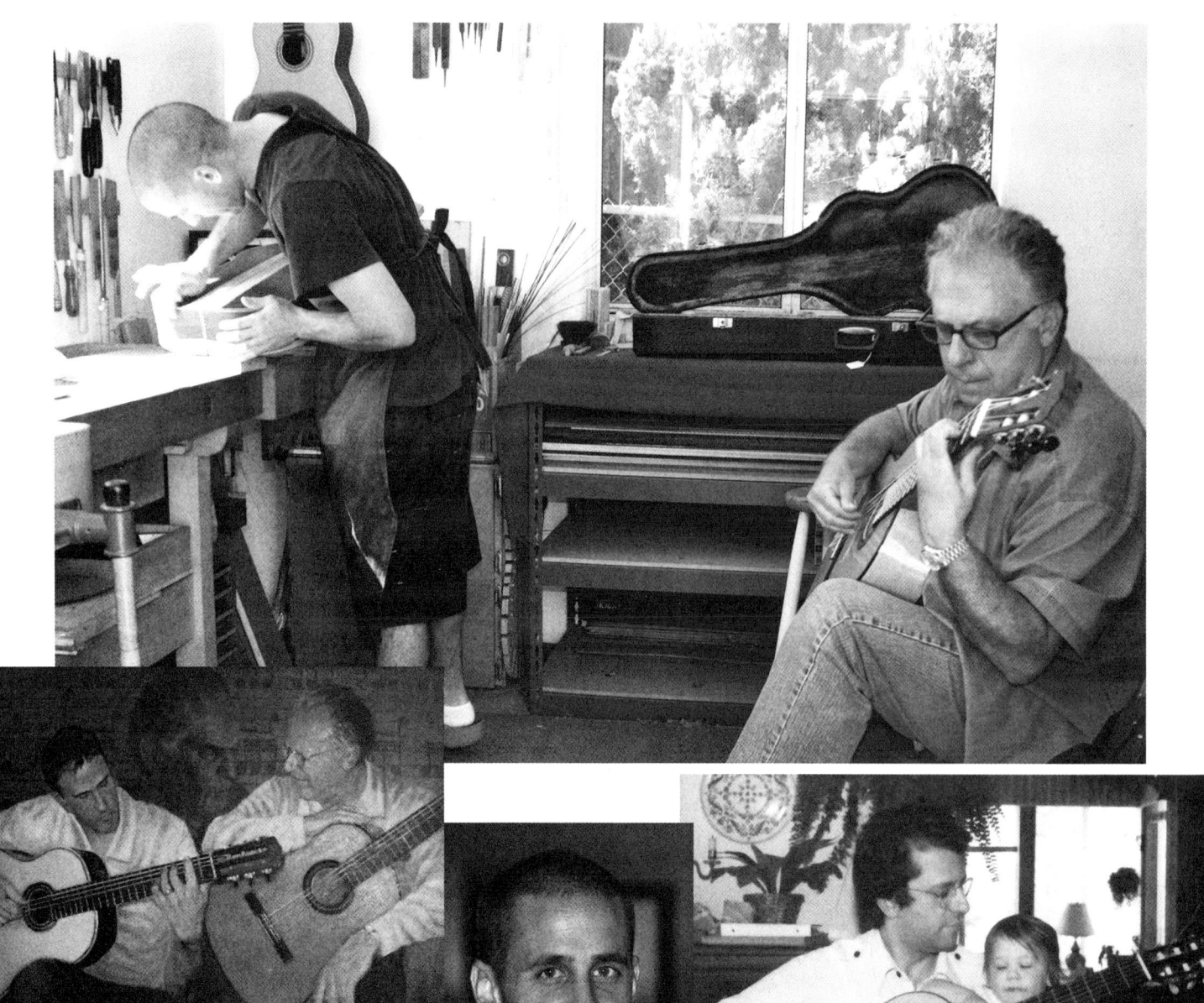

Pepe Romero, Jr., luthier.
Clockwise from above:
Pepe Jr. and Pepe in the workshop;
Father and son play together;
Pepe Jr., in the workshop of luthier Yuris Zeltins;
(center) Pepe Jr. in 2010;
a painting by Don Young depicts the three generations.
Opposite page, above: Pepe and Pepe Jr. with a sampling of
the latter's first one hundred guitars;
Below: Pepe and Pepe Jr. at a 2011 lecture demonstration
celebrating his first two hundred guitars.

Opposite page, clockwise from top: Pepe and Pepe Jr. try some guitars;
Pepe Jr. and daughter Sophia (2011); morning in the workshop;
Pepe with Pepe Jr., granddaughter Sophia, and daughter-in-law Kimberly.
This page, above left: Pepe Jr. experiences life on the road (or, more accurately, in the airports);
Pepe practices between flights;
Below: A puro *after the concert.*

Music for Solo Guitar

Ahnfelt, Oscar	*Blott en Dag (Day By Day)* (Eriksson)
Albéniz, Isaac	*Favorite Spanish Pieces (Cádiz, Córdoba, Leyenda, Rumores de la Caleta, Sevilla)* (P. Romero)
Albéniz, Isaac	*Mallorca: Barcarola, Op. 202* (Switzer/P. Romero)
Bach, J. S.	*Partita No. 2 in d minor, BWV 1004* (P. Romero)
Bach, J. S.	*Suite No. 3 in D major, BWV 1009* (P. Romero)
Barrios, Agustín	*Doce piezas para guitarra* (Amaro)
Beauvais, Wm.	*Five Lyric Pieces*
Blanchard, Harold	*Innocent Meandering* (Robinson)
Carcassi, Matteo	*Adieux à la Suisse: Tyrolienne de Bruguière variée, Op. 56* (Long)
Carulli, Ferdinando	*Variations sur l'air "Ah! vous dirai-je, Maman" ["Twinkle, Twinkle, Little Star"], Op. 60, No. 3* (Danner)
Carulli, Ferdinando	*Introduction et thème varié [on a Theme from Mozart's* The Magic Flute*], Op. 276, No. 30* (Danner)
Carulli, Ferdinando	*La Girafe à Paris: Divert. Africo-français, Op. 306* (Long)
Castellacci, Luigi	*Variations on a Theme of Paisiello: "Nel cor più non mi sento," Op. 35* (Long)
Castellacci, Luigi	*Fantaisie sur un thème viennois [A Schisserl und a Reindl], Op. 65* (Long)
Castellacci, Luigi	*Fantaisie sur la romance favorite de la* Cenerentola: *"Non più mesta" de Rossini, Op. 99* (Long)
Castellacci, Luigi	*Grande Fantaisie … sur la marche favorite de* Moïse *… de Rossini, Op. 100* (Long)
Chandler, Hugh	*Two Preludes* (Holzman)
Cimarosa, Dom.	*Three Sonatas (Nos. 15, 46, 53)* (Zohn)
Corelli, Arcangelo	*Allegro, from Violin Sonata Op. 5, No. 3* (Long)
Duarte, John W.	*Birds, Op. 66* (Goni)
Duarte, John W.	*Three Dances (Valse lyrique, Op. 137; Valse en rondeau, Op. 128; Danza eccentrica, Op. 138)*
Duarte, John W.	*Variations on an Italian Folk Song, Op. 139* (Marchione)
Duarte, John W.	*Twelve Studies, Op. 140* (De Innocentis)
Duarte, John W.	*Pequeña suite venezolana, Op. 141*
Gianoncelli, Bern.	*Tastegiata & bergamesca* (Klickstein)
Giuliani, Mauro	*Six variations sur la chanson national "I bin a Kohlbauern Bub," Op. 49* (Long)
Giuliani, Mauro	*Variazioni sulla cavatina favorita "De! Calma oh ciel" di Rossini, Op. 101* (Long)
Giuliani, Mauro	*Introduzione e variazioni sopra la cavatina favorita "Nume perdonami …" nei Baccanali di Roma, Op. 102* (Long)
Giuliani, Mauro	*Tre Tarantelle e Balletti nazionali napoletani* (King)
Gounod, Charles	*Faust Waltzes* (M. Y. Ferrer / King)
Granados, Enrique	*La Maja de Goya: Tonadilla* (P. Romero)
Handel, G. F.	*Suite for a Musical Clock* (Zohn)
Haydn, F. J.	*Sonata in G, Hob. XVI:8* (Zohn)
Horetzky, Felix	*Grandes variations, Op. 16* (Long)
Kauffman, Jay	*Juicy Fruit Shuffle*
Kauffman, Jay	*Spooky Blues*
Kauffman, Jay	*Threnody*
Kauffman, Jay	*Variations on a Mongolian Folk Song*
Kenyon, Stephen	*Maumbury Rings & Dancing Ledge*
Kenyon, Stephen	*Scottish Suite*
King, John	*Chico: Cancion andaluza*
King, John	*El Fandango rosado*
King, John	*Soledad*
King, John	*Suite for Guitar (after Salvador Dalí)*
Martín, Eduardo	*Introducción y danza*
Martín, Eduardo	*Dos Piezas: Air de paz & Son de barrio*
Melii, Pietro Paolo	*Capriccio detto "il Gran Monarca"* (Long)
Merlin, José Luis	*Dos aires pampeanos*
Merlin, José Luis	*Catedral de los pájaros*
Merlin, José Luis	*Sueño con caballos*
Merlin, José Luis	*Suite del recuerdo*
Merlin & Álvarez	*Tantanakuy: Suite argentina*

Mudarra, Alonso de	*Fantasía X* (P. Romero)
Ourkouzounov, A.	*Frammenti*
Pettoletti, Pietro	*Fantaisie sur une mélodie russe, Op. 32* (Long)
Picchianti, Luigi	*Two Arias of Rossini: Preghiera "Dal tuo stellato soglio" & Cavatina "Come dolce all'alma mia"* (Long)
Romero, Celedonio	*Tango Angelita* (P. Romero)
Romero, Pepe	*La Guitarra: A Comprehensive Study of Classical Guitar Technique and Guide to Performing*
Rossini, G. A.	*La Danza: Tarantella napolitana* (Aron)
Sagrini, Luigi	*Variations brillantes sur un thème allemand [A Schisserl und a Reindl], Op. 11* (Long)
Sagrini, Luigi	*Variations brillantes sur un air di Rossini, Op. 12* (Long)
Sanz, Gaspar	*Danzas españolas* (P. Romero)
Scarlatti, Dom.	*Sonata in a, K. 149, L. 93* (Long)
Schumann, R. A.	*Scenes from Childhood, Op. 15* (Aron)
Shields, Joseph	*Four Crucial Moments*
Sor, Fernando	*Fantaisie … dédiée à son élève Mlle Houzé* (P. Romero)
Spina, Friedrich	*Introduction et variations brillantes sur "Tu vedrai la sventurata" de Bellini, Op. 31* (Long)
Tárrega, Francisco	*El Diablo: Estudio de Sevilla* (King)
Vallet, Nicolas	*Selected Lute Works, I: Nine Preludes* (Long)
Vallet, Nicolas	*Selected Lute Works, II: Five Dances & Soet Robbert* (Long)
Vivaldi, Antonio	*Concerto in A, RV 82* (Zohn)
Wallace, Frank	*The Stubborn Oak*
Weiss, S. L.	*Ciacona* (Tornsäufer)
Weiss, S. L.	*Courante royale* (Long)
Willis, Rex	*Capriccio cantabile: Homage to Piazzolla* (Parris/Robinson)
Willis, Rex	*Two Songs of Christmas* (Robinson)

Music for Two or More Guitars

Albéniz, Isaac	*Tango in D, Op. 165, No. 2* (Long)
Bach, J. S.	*Fuga C-Dur, BWV 953* (Long)
Bach, J. S.	*Fugue in e, from Concerto e fuga, BWV 909* (Long)
Beethoven, L. van	*Duo for Two Guitars "and Eyeglasses Obbligato"* (Long/Switzer)
Oberleitner, A.	*Twelve Beer-House Ländler, Op. 10* (Long)
Rodríguez, Alberto	*Variaciones sobre un tema de W. A. Mozart*
Satie, Erik	*Enfantines* (two guitars) (Long)
Satie, Erik	*Trois Gnossiennes* (Long)
Soler, Antonio	*Sonata in e, M. 1, R. 48* (Long)
Soler, Antonio	*Sonata in D, R. 84* (Long)
Soler, Antonio	*Sonata in D, M. 34, R. 92/4* (Long)
Soler, Antonio	*Sonata in a, R. 118* (Long)
Willis, Rex	*The Floating Ancillary Ants* (for three guitars or guitar orch.)

Chamber/Vocal Music with Guitar

Aron, Stephen (ed.)	*On A Sunday Afternoon & Other American Popular Songs …* (voice and guitar)
Clement, Franz	*Variations on a Viennese Theme* (violin & guitar) (Long)
Granados, Enrique	*La Maja de Goya: Tonadilla* (voice & guitar) (P. Romero)
Kauffman, Jay	*Jinx on You* (flute & guitar)
Küffner, Joseph	*Sérénade (in D), Op. 97* (violin or flute & guitar) (Long)
Merlin, José Luis	*Evocación y joropo, from Suite del recuerdo* (guitar & flute)
Merlin, José Luis	*Progresiones para Pauline* (guitar & flute)
Merlin, José Luis	*Suite del recuerdo* (guitar & flute/violin)
Merlin, José Luis	*Suite del recuerdo* (guitar & string quartet))
Ourkouzounov, A.	*Three Folk Songs* (flute, 'cello, & two guitars)
Paganini, Nicolò	*Sonata con variazioni, M..S. 82* (violin, viola, guitar, & 'cello) (Sebastiani)
Romero, Celedonio	*Tango Angelita* (voice & guitar) (P. Romero)
Satie, Erik	*Trois Gnossiennes* (flute [violin/oboe] & guitar) (Long)
Schocker, Gary	*Hypnotized* (harp & guitar) (Kondonassis & Vieaux)
Schocker, Gary	*Mysterious Barcodes* (flute & guitar) (Vieaux)
Schocker, Gary	*Once Upon A …* (flute & guitar) (Vieaux)
Schocker, Gary	*Silkworms* (flute & guitar) (Vieaux)
Telemann, G. P.	*Trio Sonata No. 5* (rec/flute, violin, guitar, & 'cello) (Welch)
Toselli, Enrico	*Serenata, Op. 6* (violin and guitar) (Long)

Tuscany Publications

Guitaromanie Editions

Available at fine music stores everywhere, or directly from our exclusive worldwide selling agent:

The Theodore Presser Co.

588 North Gulph Road, King of Prussia, PA 19406, U.S.A.

Phone: (610) 525-3636   Fax (610) 527-7841

Web address: http://www.presser.com